NASTY!

NASTY!

EDITED BY TIFFANY SCANDAL

A KING SHOT BOOK
PDX / ATH

Nasty edited by Tiffany Scandal
First Paperback Edition

ISBN 978-0-9972518-8-3

Cover design © 2017 Matthew Revert
www.matthewrevert.com
Typeset by Michael Kazepis

King Shot Press, P.O. Box 80601, Portland, OR 97280
www.kingshotpress.com | kingshotpress@gmail.com

An extension of this copyright page appears on Page 175

100% of proceeds from this book will be donated to Planned
Parenthood, a provider of affordable healthcare, sex education
and family planning in the United States and worldwide.

CONTENTS

To all nasty women
Stay nasty

A VERY BRIEF INTRODUCTION

My hope in putting together this book was that it would serve as a sort of primer for women's issues, an introduction for the uninitiated and a fist raised in solidarity with those who understand.

I also intended for this collection to accomplish three things: raise a few bucks for Planned Parenthood, pay writers a fair wage for their work (or donate on their behalf), and provide a platform for women to share themselves.

The response has been, to say the least, humbling. During the brief submissions period, I received almost a hundred essays, and almost as many messages of support and encouragement. Much of the writing was painful to read, because of its immediacy or from drudging up long buried memories, while some pieces were so absurd or hilarious they had me laughing for hours. All of them left me feeling inspired.

Planned Parenthood—if you don't already know—provides *affordable* healthcare, sex education, and family planning. This is especially important to folks with little or no means. Because even if you've got no money, no insurance, they'll still help you.

When I was in college, the services provided by the university clinic weren't always that great or professional—don't even get me started on a particular Plan B debacle I experienced. The local Planned Parenthood, on the other hand, always took me in and provided prompt pap smears, cancer screenings, STI testing, and patiently talked with me about birth control options. (I used to get really angry, intense periods.) Being broke, like many students, it was a great relief that most of these services were provided free of charge. Because of this I believe that it's important to try and help pay this much-needed help forward, especially as reproductive rights continue to be under attack across the country.

I aimed to capture here conversations about race, gender, sexuality, means, and various other angles of struggle. And while these voices may be unified in their ownership of identity, in their individual "nastiness," they're also at times self-critical and reflective. Feminism is a work-in-progress, and I tried to make sure every piece of writing in this book underscores and is consistent with that interpretation.

It was also important that this anthology feature work that was written exclusively by women. All too often allies and advocates can unintentionally, and sometimes intentionally, shut women down without ever letting us finish speaking our side. In this book you will find no such silence. These are women telling stories only they can tell, uninterrupted. By having purchased this book that's in your hands, you've helped make that happen, and for that I thank you.

Tiffany Scandal
January 2018

M O N S T E R

MISSY SUICIDE

"If you want to make a human being a
monster, deny them, at the cultural level,
any reflection of themselves."
—JUNOT DIAZ

Growing up I felt like a monster. I didn't see anyone who
looked like me. No dark-haired girls with glasses and
freckles and long noses were on my TV or billboards. There
was no place where I felt I belonged. I couldn't play sports.
I sucked at math. I was not popular enough to get asked
to dances and the suburban picket fence future seemed as
unwelcoming as high school.

So I embraced becoming a monster, I used it as
protection, relished in it. If I was a monster, I would be the
scariest fucking monster a 5' soft-spoken girl could be. I
put metal in my face and dyed my hair unnatural hues and
gave myself fucked up haircuts. I wore black and ill-fitting
clothes. Punk rock and literature became my salvation.
The outsider is the tragic hero of all great stories. My
heroes were Holden Caulfield, PonyBoy Curtis and Dean
Moriarty. My life would be a tragic fuck you that would

make all of them sorry that they wasted my potential. A girl could dream, kind of.

There were no female protagonists of the books that I read or the music I listened to. Girls were mostly absent. When they were included, at best they were mysterious beauties; at worst they were cruel tormentors or shrewish bitches whose only pleasure in life was inflicting pain. My literary view of women, coupled with the realities of high school girl hierarchy, painted my sex and, by proxy myself, in a not very positive light.

High school was a beautiful disaster, but then I went to college, lucked into a career that suited me and I found a support system. Things got better.

Until they didn't.

Your 20's are a fucking rollercoaster. Seriously. Try to enjoy the ride and know that you are strong enough to get through it.

I found myself back in Portland, lost and sad, with no plan and no where to fit in. Feeling more like a monster than I had ever before. Maybe because I was so sad and hopeless, I could see through my tear stained glasses that there were lots of other monsters like me. And they were beautiful.

I wanted to create a space where they could see each other. I wanted to hold a mirror up to my fellow monsters so that they could see that they were gorgeous just the way that they were. We didn't have to play into the narrative we were given. We weren't the bitchy shrew or the mysterious tormentor. We didn't have to play into high school girl competition. Maybe if we shared our stories with one another, we could be the hero of our own great stories. So I created SuicideGirls.

And people came. People shared their stories and became the mirrors for other girls to see themselves and what they can become. The sense of hope and pride and belonging that I have because of this community bolsters me every day. I am so grateful to everyone for being there, sharing and supporting each other and unabashedly being themselves.

There are almost 3,000 SuicideGirls and hundreds of thousands of hopefuls from every continent including Antarctica. We are many. We are strong. We don't need to fit in to their stories. We have our own and they are more interesting.

FUCKING FAT

SABRINA DROPKICK

The first time I considered that my body could maybe, possibly not be as gross as I had been led to believe was when I discovered April Flores, the fire-engine-red-headed BBW porn goddess.

I had always disassociated during sex and masturbation. I needed to emotionally detach myself from my "unacceptable" body in order to cum—otherwise, I'd be hyper-aware of the "fact" that I wasn't sexually appealing, and I'd be shamed back into my clothes, or worse, into a somewhat paralytic state until my partner was finished. I'd even been rejected during sex when a "friend" with "benefits" shamed me for being too insecure to get on top. Like, he got seriously angry and left the bed to go check his fucking Facebook on his stupid fucking desktop computer. We pretty much sat in naked silence until I mustered up the confidence to leave.

(Btdubs, I quoted "friends" and "benefits" not because I object to this type of relationship or anything—friends with benefits can totally be safe and healthy—but because this motherfucker obviously did not care for or respect me as a friend, and I benefitted fucking nothing from our nights together—except maybe the last time I saw him, which was also my last night in Chicago before moving to LA. Only then did he actually take me out and pay for my meal.)

I first became aware that something was "wrong" with my body in sixth grade. I had just transitioned from glitter hair gel and boy bands into baggy UFO pants and pop punk, and I had the biggest fucking crush on this dopey skater kid. I showed my BFF how I'd written his name over and over and over and over and over again in my Spongebob journal, only for her to get way too excited and take it upon herself to play matchmaker. I was sitting on the steps to the front entrance of our school when she returned with The Verdict: He didn't like-like me, and she wouldn't dish the deets until I asked her like, a million times. She finally looked away to say, "He said you're cool and everything, but he can't date you. . . because you're too fat."

It's almost as if that one incident is what burst the bubble of body-shaming bullshit and opened up the vortex of Patriarchal Beauty Standards™, because from there I . . .

- Spent a string of summers living off of generic toaster waffles and spray butter because my mom bribed me with clothes, shoes, and then just straight up cash to lose weight;
- Began concealing as much skin as possible, even wearing layers and hoodies through the muggy-as-fuck summers of my Philadelphia hometown;

• Stopped wearing bathing suits in exchange for oversized t-shirts and men's shorts that reached my knees;
• Accepted the advances of a heroin addict nearly twice my age because he was the first boy, I mean, man to ever make a pass at me;
• Stayed in that super toxic and emotionally draining relationship for three years because I was afraid there would never be another person who'd, you know, like-like me again.

Then, during my freshman year at Columbia College Chicago, I found that video of April Flores. She was fucking a "mechanic" and he actually, like, fucked all of her. Like, not just a bang, flip, and finish, but he passionately kissed her, her body, caressed her curves and rolls with care and desire. I really believed that he thought she was hot. I believed that she believed she was hot. And though our bodies are equally unique, I saw shapes similar to mine and began to consider that maybe I could believe in my body in this way, too.

I wish I could call that my big fat fairy tale ending. I wish I could say that April Flores served as Queen of the royal empire of fat acceptance, leading me on a chariot of dicks through the peaks and valleys of my journey towards self-love and empowerment, finally reaching the nirvana of body positivity where we rejoiced amongst a new dimension where no one body was alike, every size and shape was celebrated, and we lived happily ever after in eternal big bitch bliss.

But I can't.

I decided to try a full contact sport when I was 22. I'd never been involved in any sort of physical activity beyond the mother-daughter Curves membership we had for like, a year (if that). My mom was quick to remind me of this when I called to tell her that I joined a roller derby league. She kinda laughed. "You know that's a sport, right?"

Roller derby changed my fucking life and it's still a driving force of my well-being and identity five years later. When I joined, though, I was still a few years shy of accepting my place in addiction recovery, as well as finally being properly diagnosed with bipolar II. An addictive personality gave me obsessively sharp focus while mania provided unending energy which fueled my weekly routine of two to three derby practices, three to four crossfit classes, usually an outdoor skate or two, and eventually I'd pick up paleo eating, which really meant that if I didn't feel like cooking, or if I was out and there were no paleo options, then I just didn't eat.

I gotta say, I don't blame derby for this, and this isn't how I hit the ground running off the bat. I lost 30 pounds in my first few months just by showing up to practice and maybe skating the Orange Line bike path once a week. I didn't change my eating habits, but I did begin to explore self-expression through fashion. On the track I wasn't Sabrina, I was #215 Philly Sleazesteak, and this sort of persona gave me enough chutzpah to step over my insecurities and into a crop top.

There was one slight hiccup the first day I showed up to practice in a crop top, when a head coach (the only man in our league at the time) chewed through a few excuses as to why I shouldn't be allowed to wear one. He was quickly shut down by one of the two other plus-size skaters, noting that many of the smaller girls wore even less clothes on the track. Other than that, though, I've never personally experienced body shaming in roller derby, whether it's at home or during our travels. In fact, it's become the exact community and support system I was so hungry for since moving to LA a few years prior.

So naturally, when I started to inadvertently lose weight, my league mates responded with what most would consider encouragement and support. Oh my god, have you lost weight? You look so good! You're getting so skinny! Wow, have you lost even more weight? What's your secret!

You guise. I literally, in my whole fucking life, had never, ever, ever, ever, ever, ever, EVER had ANYONE say ANYTHING even remotely nice about my body, unless you count the million times I've been complimented on my fucking eye lashes. If I could roll my eyes any harder, they'd fall the fuck off.

Even though I came into my body confidence years earlier at nearly 300 pounds, receiving this type of attention for the first time became totally addicting. It's true. There's really no other way to describe it. Once I tasted mainstream approval, I could not resist it. It became unmanageable and out of my control. I lost a total 100 pounds way too fucking fast.

When we finally got our own rink, I quit crossfit because the schedule conflicted with our now surplus of practices . . . and I gained a teeny bit of weight. Then I got a boyfriend and gained a little more weight. Then I lost that boyfriend and gained some more. Had a depressive episode, gained weight. Got injured, gained weight. More depressive episodes, gained weight. Then I got SUPER fucking injured, got in and out of an abusive relationship, got super sick, needed surgery, and was out of derby for a year. In that year, I relapsed and hit my longest, most damaging depressive episode in my life. When I finally "woke up," I realized that my clothes didn't fit anymore. I was 300 pounds again, except this time, I was not okay with it.

Depression and addiction are pretty fucking gnarly—I know, I'm sure you would've never guessed. But seriously, I hit my final bottom so hard, it knocked my fucking noggin right out, and this big monster called Life just stomped all over it, broke it down into its most minimal state until it was totally unrecognizable, then handed me the pieces to put back together by myself. Some of the pieces were still there, but some of them weren't even mine, and some of them I can't say where the fuck they came from 'cause they were just blank.

Right now, I'm about a year to the month since waking up. We found the right cocktail of pills that have kept me stable for the longest period of time since I was 12. I took my one year chip in June. I organized the first San Fernando Valley Zine Fest. I've got a grad school interview next week. From the outside, most people think I'm fuckin' killin' it, especially considering that just 15 months ago I "voluntarily" checked into an inpatient psych facility. But I gotta tell ya, those pieces aren't even close to being put back together yet. And one of those missing pieces is my fearless confidence, especially about my size.

I still wasn't feeling completely 100 when I dipped back into the dating scene last year, but I did it anyway, and on my first date I found myself reverting back to my middle school tendency of shielding my body with layers of cotton, polyester, and denim skin. Look, even though I know my denim vest is pretty fucking cool, the truth is that the only reason it even became a staple in my wardrobe was because it's stiff enough to mask my shape.

This time, though, hiding didn't feel so good, so I begrudgingly borrowed a page from my last cognitive behavioral outpatient program and decided to utilize contrary action. Since I'd always used clothes as a method to hide, I needed to step out from the shadows and make it the staple of my self-care. "If clothes make me feel bad," I thought, "then I guess I gotta make them feel good."

•

How do we manage wounds? We tear the fucking bandage off. Let it breathe. Let the air sculpt it into a scab. We have to push ourselves through the discomfort as our flesh is replenished, and we can't fucking touch it until it sheds itself to reveal shiny new skin. I guess I could have also just said that instead of avoidance, the more we engage, the less we fear. I revisited crop tops, conquered the high-waisted look, then moved on to a bathing suit, a romper, and now I'm working on shorts. . . In half a year, I've conquered five times the "fatshion" that I had embraced before—before the relapse, before the injury, before the weight gain and the weight loss. Even when I thought I had my pieces together, I could never wear that kinda shit.

I was watching fat porn recently when I realized, "Hey, this girl's belly rolls just like mine, and this other girl's proportions aren't "right" just like mine. . . so if I think their bodies are gorgeous as fuck, then why can't I feel that way about mine?"

The date I mentioned earlier has actually become the relationship that I stand by today. And no matter how much he swooned for me, calling me beautiful on the fucking daily, poppin' boners even at the mention of my butt, I was incapable of believing it. Our sex life was totally dampened by my insecurities. I couldn't be present or enjoy it in the moment because I was so wrapped up in how things jiggled, what position offered what angle and whether that angle was flattering or not.

Then one day I plopped into my bed for a self fuck fest when I reached for my iPad to find it was dead. I can't fucking stand watching any form of media entertainment on my phone, so watching porn was just not an option that day. I looked over at my fuck basket of condoms and lube and vibrators, and none of that was really appealing to my va-jee either. I zoned out in disappointment and caught myself in a dead-eyed gaze when I re-focused my vision to see the chair beside my vanity. It's really just an old drummer's seat in front of a dresser with a big ol' trash-picked mirror on top of it, but whatever, it works, and the mirror really is big as fuck. Like, it almost reaches my ceiling.

So my pants-less ass got out of bed and perched my right foot up on the seat so that the mirror reflected everything from my Golan the Insatiable thigh tattoo and up. I pulled my t-shirt up to reveal the two pale, doughy rolls that form my tummy. It looked just fucking like that girl's tum in the porn! Except mine is kissed with ink, "Fatty Fatale" permanently scribbled across my top roll in an arch above my belly button.

Sans toys or partner, this led to what was probably the quickest, hardest orgasm I'd ever had since being a pre-teen queer kid after discovering *Suicide Girls*.

I guess I said all that to say this: It's fucking okay to not be okay. I've felt a lot of shame about my shame, which is a totally fucked up inception of feels. I paraded around with the body-positive flag for years before suddenly finding it ripped from my hands and replaced with repulsion. I felt fucking awful about it. I felt like I lost my credibility as a fat activist. I felt like I lost my whole fucking identity.

But just as it took radical self-expression to discover self-love, it's now taking radical acceptance to maintain it. Whether it's challenging societal expectations for the way fat bodies should dress or simply fucking yourself, the most important part about finding genuine pleasure in our bodies is to do it on our own terms, with no strings attached to anyone's expectations, not even those assumed for us champions of size acceptance. We are allowed to have intricate journeys along bumpy roads; to have bad days, bad weeks, and bad months. Sorry not sorry, but we're all just like, imperfect human beings or whatever.

PS: There's no way I can talk about self-acceptance without quoting the one person who's said best: "If you can't love yourself, how in the hell you gonna love somebody else?"

I don't fucking know, RuPaul, but I do know that I'll always keep trying.

B U D D Y
ROCKET

It's getting late on a beautiful summer night. The club is rowdy. The crowd is having fun. It's wall-to-wall sweaty people waiting in line for drinks and the bartenders are working their asses off. The security guy has propped the door open to let in some cool air. The owner and his cronies have just rolled up on their motorcycles. People are clinking glasses and throwing money around. Women are sitting on their boyfriend's laps at the stage and cheering wildly as each dancer takes her turn.

I'm making my rounds, jumping from table to table, hustling my heart out during what I call "The Golden Hour," which is the hour before the club closes when people are drunk and ready to spend.

I'm determined to send them all home with empty wallets.

Another dancer and I pair up at this time of night. It's easier for us to hustle big groups when we work together. We joke with bachelor parties and birthday groups, convincing them to buy dances for each other with the two of us. When we return from the private dance room with one guy, all we have to say is, "Who's next?" to keep them spending. We're excellent at this.

As the owner and his friends settle into the club, it's only polite to take a few minutes to say hi. I grab my drink and walk over. He smiles and waves. I know what he likes when it comes to dancers—either twenty-one year olds who let him take body shots off their flat stomachs, or dancers who blast his club on social media and bring in paying customers. I certainly wasn't that first type, so I made sure I was the second. I advertised his club and my shifts every night I worked, and I had regular customers to show for it. I pushed him to put me on the glossy advertisements and I did everything I could to promote myself and his business. Beyond that, I kept him at arm's length. But that only made him want to chat with me more; especially after a few drinks.

"Hey did you see that Cleo was just in here?" he laughed. "She wants night shifts again, but she's been doing this gig for too long." He changed his voice to sound like a haggard old woman, "Can I come back and work here again pleeeeeease?"

I didn't respond. Cleo was my friend, I'd worked with her for years, and he knew that. I found it telling that he was mocking a woman he used to date, and who was only three years older than he and I were. Maybe he didn't realize that I talked to Cleo all the time, and that I knew the last time she worked here a month ago he hit on her relentlessly. She told me he'd cornered her at the bar and kept trying to kiss her, but she wasn't having it. Sounds like somebody was sore that he got rejected.

I changed the subject, determined to keep it positive. "I'm so glad Leah is back. I love her. Where did she tour, do you know?"

I pointed at the gorgeous woman on stage. She'd taken a working road trip (or as strippers like to say: a paycation) and had just returned to Portland and her regular night shifts at the club.

"Oh yeah, I don't know. Uhh, somewhere down south. New Orleans I think? She lost some weight, did you see? She looks good. She's been doing yoga, it really slimmed her down." He tore his eyes from the stage and looked over at me. He grinned devilishly and it made me uneasy. "Maybe you should do some yoga, buddy!" he quipped and reached his right hand to grip the side of my waist.

I stood there for a moment, stunned. I'm five feet eight inches tall and I weigh 140 pounds. Though I am certainly not small, I am toned and healthy. There is absolutely nothing wrong with the way I look, thank you very much. I gave him a hard, cold look and let the silence of this awkward moment linger; hoping it made him incredibly uncomfortable. As my mama said, never let them see you sweat. I picked up my drink. "I have people waiting for dances. See ya." I walked away with my shoulders pushed back and my head high.

A week later, he and his friends were back on their motorcycles. The weather was balmy, and the dancers were hanging out on the front bar patio in only bra and panties under the streetlight, causing cars to suddenly slow as they drove by. Slack-jawed men gaped from their open windows. Some whistled and honked. Motorcycle rides were offered by the boss man. Every few minutes he'd cruise around a few blocks with a scantily clad dancer on the back of his bike. Normally, I'd say no. I grew up around motorcycles and they don't impress me that much. He didn't seem to know how to handle it with the kind of confidence I'd want as a passenger. Besides, if I'm gonna ride a motorcycle, I'd rather it be on a dirt trail or going fast; preferably both. But today I obliged. Swinging a long leg over the back of the seat, I shouted, "My turn! Let's go."

He nodded.

As he pulled out into the road, I reached my arms around his body. He was wearing a helmet, so I tested the volume of my voice by yelling, "Hey can you hear me?"

He nodded. "Yeah I can," his reply muffled by the helmet.

We weren't going very fast. The speed limit was low and the traffic was thick.

"Hey didn't you say you started going to the gym?" I asked. I imagined his confused look; this wasn't the normal conversation he had with girls on the back of his motorcycle. The warm wind whipped my hair back and I smiled.I had him trapped. I shifted my grip on his waist so that both of my hands were reaching as far forward as possible. Then I grabbed the bulk of his beer belly and squeezed hard, moving it up and down, rolls jiggling in my grip. He couldn't move; he had to steer the motorcycle.

"You really gotta lay off those Voodoo Doughnuts, buddy." I yelled.

We were going faster now and headed back to the club. I knew he heard me, but he didn't reply. I felt his shoulders tense up. I didn't care that I could have all of my shifts taken away at his whim. This was worth it. We rolled up and parked. The next dancer excitedly waited for her turn. I hopped off and gave him a boy scout salute and wicked grin. "Thanks for the ride, man."

HOW TO ACCEPT THAT YOU ARE TRANSGENDER IN 11 EASY STEPS

MP JOHNSON

Step 1: Stand in the middle of the playground and realize that you're not a boy. You're a girl. You're definitely a girl. Realize this as only a kid can—in a convoluted mess of thoughts and feelings that you don't have words for and never will. Keep playing with He-Man guys. Don't tell anyone.

Step 2: Stay home sick from school one day and see a daytime talk show that has transgender women as guests. Maybe it's a, "Which One of These Beautiful Women Is Really a Dude?" episode. Maybe it's a, "Help! My Husband Wants to Become a Lady!" episode. Feel your guts churn at the combination of relief that comes when you see trans women on the screen and realize, "OMG that's me!" and horror in the fact that they are on the show to be gawked and laughed at. Recognize that the world doesn't want you.

Don't tell anyone.

Step 3: When you get the Internet, immediately search "transgender." See that the search results are mostly porn, because that's how the Internet worked then. Look at the websites anyway, because at least it's something, right? Let your confusion mix with your raging hormones and flush your quest to understand yourself into a swirling pool of sexual attraction to what you are seeing on the screen, making the whole situation even messier. Feel ashamed. Don't tell anyone.

Step 4: Shoplift makeup. Shoplift skirts. Compromise your morals because everything you have seen has convinced you that committing crimes is more socially acceptable than being transgender. Get caught and create an elaborate story for your parents about how you were stealing this stuff on a dare. Don't tell anyone.

Step 5: Start lifting weights. Listen to super macho music. Get into fights. Do everything possible to convince yourself you are man. Throw away all the makeup. Throw away all the skirts. They don't fit anymore anyway. Bulk up. Flex in the mirror. Hate what you see. Don't tell anyone.

Step 6: Accept that you are a crossdresser. You are not a woman. You are a man with a fun little hobby that you can skip school and do, that you can skip work and do. Dress up. Get pretty. Look in the mirror when you're done and feel a level of comfort and honesty that you can't even really grasp. Ask yourself, okay, what do I do now? Sit around. Do nothing. Feel like yourself, but super bored, super alone. Undress and wash it all off. Feel guilt that you can't understand. Hate yourself. Look longingly at knives. Don't tell anyone.

Step 7: Repeat Step 5. A lot.

Step 8: Go on secret crossdressing trips to places like New York and LA. Stay at scary motels. Make plans with other crossdressers online. Avoid emails from the ones who just want to come to your hotel for sex. Realize this isn't about sex for you. Wish it was, because then maybe you could be happy just dressing up and fucking in random hotel rooms. But you cannot, and the crossdressers who say they want to go out will only go to crossdressing bars, not punk rock shows, and then ditch you anyway because they are understandably afraid to go out into the world, so go to the punk rock shows anyway. Stand alone wishing for someone to talk to you. Feel somehow even more alone. Spend the rest of the trip eating pizza naked on your hotel bed and wondering how many sleeping pills would make this all go away. Go back home and act like everything is perfectly normal. Don't tell anyone.

Step 9: Fall in love with drag. Practice this style of makeup and dress. Go out. Perform. When friends ask what's up, act like it's just for show, just about the art form. Just act like it's no big deal. Convince yourself that you can be a drag queen, and that you can express yourself—your full self—through that persona on an occasional basis. Realize that drag is a work-intensive art form, and that you do not have time to do the work. Keep telling yourself that you will. Keep telling yourself that this is good enough. Don't tell anyone.

Step 10: Make vague posts about your gender on social media. Come out as non-binary. Say that you are neither male nor female, because somehow, you think this will be easier on people than if you just admit you're female. Then say that you are feminine-leaning non-binary, which you're pretty sure you've just made up. Post pictures of yourself in cute clothes and a little makeup. Get headaches trying to convince yourself that you cannot be defined by the gender binary, all the while knowing that you have always been female. Don't tell anyone.

Step 11: Come out as transgender, not because you are brave, but because you have spent 40 years being versions of you that you know full well are not you. Because you have tried every fucking other option and are desperate to just be honest with yourself and the people you care about. Because the thought of living another fucking day in hiding hurts more at this point than every possible repercussion that you could face upon coming out. Tell everyone.

A BLACK TYPE OF FEMINISM

CERVANTE POPE

For most of my life, I never considered myself a feminist. Not because I disagreed with the movement—quite the opposite, actually. But growing up, "feminist" and "feminism" were never terms thrown around in my single-parent home. My mother, a reformed Jehovah's Witness raised in the deepest trenches of the Creole South during a time where schools were newly integrated, surely never defined herself that way either. It always seemed that despite how she, the youngest of nearly three handfuls of children, chose to verbally interpret herself, the power within her wasn't actually hers. It belonged to those older, stronger and thought to be wiser.

She raised me with that same mode of thinking.

It was confusing witnessing a real time fragility that so heavily contrasted the things she said, along with the stereotypes of black women drilled into my brain on tv. She would tell me to always be a "strong black woman," much like the loud, no-nonsense black women that Hollywood portrays as the ones not to fuck with. I remember a few times growing up where my mother's confidence as a female radiated as this character trope though typically, she was a conscious victim to a world where men—in particular, white ones—ruled everything. How bright we shined as women, as black women especially, would never matter. Or at least, that's what she would say to me when submitting was simpler than confrontation. . . which was often.

Numerous jobs had screwed her over as had numerous men she once called lovers. To her, that was just her lot in life. A lot that I would soon be immersed in myself. Her only real advice to me was to marry rich, as love meant nothing but control; having to work so hard to barely have the same as everyone else did was fruitless. Even as a child I understood this to be easier said than done, and easier to desire than actually have.

Of myself I knew of certain facts to be true: I'm of color, I'm a woman, and I come from a family with essentially no financial stability or institution. That meant that ahead of me laid a road of incredibly hard work for nothing, or tirelessly searching for a man to fit into my mother's box of worthiness. The thought of having such a lack of control over my own life because of my race, sex and class depressed me, but complacency with "the system" was almost hereditary in this sense. That slowly changed the older I grew, but entirely changed once I moved to Portland.

With almost no knowledge of Portland at all, I stepped

off my plane into pouring rain. The people passing by were tatted, pierced and carried themselves with a general sense of self confidence I personally lacked. I soon began yet another journey into an assimilated life. Everyone here was so radical, so non-fearing in their stances and beliefs, my pretty traditional upbringing was immediately challenged. I welcomed that, though seeing such a comfort in nonconformity was somewhat jarring. I had always been different in my own way; my tastes, aesthetically and musically, much different than what was assumed for someone of color to enjoy. That was my kind of rebellion, but I soon grew to realize that feminism itself is a form of rebellion.

I had gone from essentially no exposure to feminism to drowning in it. The reality of my sheltered upbringing pretty much served to me on a platter of social media posts and callout culture. The confusing facet in this, at least six years ago when I first moved here, was that gender and sexual identity were placed on a higher pedestal than race. As someone whose existence is a Venn diagram of all these aspects, I felt as though I had to choose between which one was of most importance. Struggling with that selection placed me in situations where all aspects where challenged, threatened and ultimately suffered.

Quite often, I found myself slightly fetishized. Not only by white partners, but by white friends as well. In this vanilla sea of a city, I had to confront how heavy nature and nurture weighed in my decision making. How much I'd continue to let expectations overrun who I felt I was. Understandably, I had soon grown tired of being the "starter black girl" for white men, or the "black dictionary" for my friends. The amount of emotional labor it took to love and care for all these different people was too much, so when I met D.S., I thought things would be different. I couldn't have been more wrong.

D.S. was older, sensitive and creatively talented. White, yes, but in a way I found accessible and easy to deal with. He was from the East Coast and had an understanding of hard life in a way that, at times, related to mine, but also in different ways I felt I could learn from. He played in a band I liked before we even met, though that had little to do with what drew me to him. He was vulnerable in ways that a man hadn't been with me before, and that warmed me. But my fancy for him eventually turned into a pattern of emotionally exploitative behavior that took me entirely too long to face.

I should mention that D.S. had some mental illnesses about him. Ones that made it hard for him to see in the moment exactly how abusive his words and behavioral tendencies could be. Sometimes, he'd attack my womanhood if I disagreed with him, saying his lover should always be on his side. Other times, he'd criticize me sexually, which of course led back to my position as a woman. He chastised the term "cis," yet had very "cis" expectations of his partner. Those things, I set aside, thinking to myself that a man, like any other person, has the right to want whatever he wants out of a partner. None of that had stopped me from loving him. I let him move in with me when he needed. I stood by his side through dramatic situations that arose out his past. When forced to choose between certain career opportunities and his wishes, I almost always put his wishes first.

I, by all definitive means, was a supportive woman.

I hadn't yet realized how hypnotized I was by what I

perceived to be fairness. As bad as those instances were, the worst came through an intersectional crux of my sex, gender roles and race. As if being a woman of color in Trump's America, hell, in ANY America wasn't hard enough, the one person I thought I could rely on turned on me.

Portland, in all of its progressive-leaning ideals, isn't all that progressive at all. Sure, the hipsters, the oogles, and the weed-puffing-hippies—for the most part—participate in the equality of all beings. Participation here is often expressed through actively not being racist or sexist, without the clearest grasp that microaggressions and subconscious thoughts are still participatory acts. D.S.'s part in all this came as a surprise to me, since I thought he was very much unlike the others.

During a weekend of free speech rallies and protests, I found myself doused in the defeat of what I thought would be a simple conversation. D.S. mentioned to me his disdain for Portland's "radical leftists" protesting against the alt-right and free-speechers; claiming that, in so many words, the latter groups had a right to feel the way they feel because hate speech "is" a part of free speech.

Needless to say, I was shocked.

For someone who I spent so much time and energy on to say that to me, I couldn't comprehend what I had just heard. He'd seen me go through instances of both racism and sexism. He claimed to have had my back no matter what, yet had been fostering such a problematic viewpoint. I was nothing shy of livid.

In the moments that followed this conversation, my reaction garnered one from him that went entirely too far. I tried my best, as does any person of color trying to convey sensitive points like this to a white person, to make the lightbulb of, "oh shit, I should probably shut up," go off in his head. Instead, what should have ended with an apology ended with a threat.

I told D.S. that as a cis white man, his opinions on this matter aren't as important as those directly affected by it (i.e. women and women-identifying persons and people of color). The lightbulb of knowledge I expected to turn on ended up becoming a full blown explosion of misogynistic workings.

D.S. proceeded to call me a racist and a fascist. Claiming that I've laid down with Portland's alt-right and "dangerous" feminist movement, and that I am no better than the people allies are protesting against. He then blasted me on social media, spreading lies in attempts to smear my identity. But none of that was as bad as his claim to know what it was like to be discriminated against because of the color of his skin, all because of my calling him out.

Many who observed the crumbling of our relationship online came to my defense, most of them women or persons who identified as such. All of this led to violent threats against himself, those in my life, and me. For the first time since our relationship began, I was concerned for my safety. But even with this fear, my heart couldn't help but swell with love.

Despite all of his completely misguided ramblings, he happened to be right about one thing—I did find myself siding with an interpretation of feminism that was never instilled in me before. I had never experienced that level of support before; from women I considered friends, and people I looked up to in one way or another. Be it for their particular strength of conviction, their talent, or some combination of those things and more, I wasn't expecting to have anyone jump to my defense. I was so used to being a one-woman army warring on the battle lines of life, that to finally see that I had a female battalion behind me the whole time was a welcomed relief. What I gained out of this pretty traumatic experience led to something more beautiful than I had ever imagined.

With the relationship clearly over, I worked through the brunt of my feelings with these female counterparts. Though the healing process is one that seldom comes quickly or easy, I've already a newfound appreciation, not only for myself, but for the inspiring women around me. Their support motivated me to stop letting a man's definition of love dictate my definition of myself. I've since made many positive changes in my life that have led me to carry myself with an air self-love and confidence I didn't know I had in me.

As with any movement, modern and extreme feminism has its faults. But what I've come to realize is that it's a term not necessarily meant to expound or constrict anyone's identity, but one to serve as elemental clarification. It's a term paralleling support. The truest contemporary feminists don't use it as a means to put down, alienate or judge others no matter how they identify. Ideally, it should do for everyone what it did for me—uplift, validate and facilitate some of the most strong-willed beings on Earth.

A YEAR IN THE LIFE OF A SAD AMERICAN LIBERAL

JULIE REA

JULY 2016 — JUNE 2017

July 24, 2016

This was my first day volunteering at the 2016 Democratic National Convention. On my way there, I witnessed this giant hawk have a heatstroke. It fell out of the sky and landed in a heap on the sidewalk, about fifteen feet away from where I was boarding the bus.

The bird was the size of our twenty-pound house cat, its wings draped around its unmoving body like a blanket. Wind blew the bird's tail feathers and exposed its legs, yellow cables tipped with splayed talons.

The bus driver sprang from the bus with his water bottle and poured water next to the head of the unmoving bird. After a minute or so, the bird flopped on its back. Some in the gathering crowd cheered. The bus driver poured water on the hawk's big chest. The hawk rolled back upright and raised its head.

The bus driver left the crowd and returned to the bus. As the bus pulled out of the terminal, I saw people taking selfies with their faces about a foot away from the hawk's gigantic head, its beak opening and closing as the hawk drank from another guy's water bottle.

Everybody at the convention was cheerful, even the Bernie Sanders protestors. This despite the fact that being outside in Philadelphia feels like wearing a hot, wet wool blanket. One person marching in protest was wearing a full furry rat suit; I hope he survived.

The DNC had pins for the volunteers, and I was told to hand them out. The other person on pin duty was a former CEO who looked fifty-something but told me she was in her seventies. She asked if she could photograph me as part of a project in which she takes pictures of women and displays them in her bathroom so that she "can appreciate beauty in aging." I'm not terribly aged, but I guess she found my wheelchair, tattoo, and fancy red boots interesting in some related way.

August 16, 2016

Today I went discount shopping and found a great dress. But when I got it in my hands, I saw the Ivanka Trump label. I dropped it on the floor in a surprised convulsion.

It was like that time we forgot about some potatoes stored in a rarely used cupboard. One day, I opened the cupboard door to an unexpected jungle of sprouted potatoes, and I shrieked in startled dismay.

Finding my hands full of an Ivanka Trump dress was like that, somehow.

September 5, 2016
My hairdresser of close to ten years told me that she was sick of people who receive disability who don't deserve it. I got anxious because I receive disability. Her scissors were flashing around my head, and I didn't feel up to challenging her assumptions.

She's voting Trump, in part because of the undeserving disability recipients.

October 25, 2016
We have a big window in our living room that looks out onto a row of little houses. Traditionally, the houses try to outdo one another with decorations during the holidays. Now, all the houses are Halloween-themed, with orange lights and jack-o-lanterns and paper skeletons and all that.

Except for one house. This one house has a Trump/Pence sign and a giant flag. Nothing more.

September 30, 2016
Therapy session following the first presidential debate:

Me: After the debate Monday, that feeling of black despair that I've been talking about has lifted.

Psychiatrist: We still have six weeks to go. I heard today that the Ohio county that has been the bellwether for every election ever is leaning Trump.

Me: :(

November 9, 2016

Yesterday, I voted, went to work, came home, turned off my phone and went to bed at 8:30. Woke up at 3:30 AM, saw the front page of the New York Times online with the headline about Trump's win in font the size of an announcement of the end of the world. For several moments, I wasn't sure what was real. Started making calls, waking up people who'd just gone to bed.

Later, on my way home from work, I was riding in a SEPTA elevator with an elderly black woman who looked as miserable as I felt. There we were, two frail people riding in an elevator with pee on the floor, looking like somebody had killed our dogs.

I felt like a shit person for being white. And I wanted this sad-looking black woman to know that I felt her pain. So, I said, out of the blue like a crazy person, "I didn't vote for him."

The lady lost her look of sadness. "I did," she said with a kind of wrathful victory. "He's going to wipe out abortions in this Godless country!"

I went home and smoked cigarettes for the first time in two years.

November 15, 2016

I love our bathroom. I spend many quality moments in the giant bathtub, read in the bath, make important decisions there.

I had a nightmare last night. In my dream, I was in the bathroom about to take a bath, looked in the tub, and found it half-full of mud and sewage.

November 17, 2016

My brother J. lives in Harlem. Somebody saw his lily whiteness and mistook him for a Trump supporter, challenged him, and the thing ended with the somebody declaring it was "Donald Trump time" and suggesting that my brother be taken around the block and beaten up.

November 25, 2016

I got rip-roaring wasted on beet vodka over Thanksgiving dinner with R. and my brother J. and his family. I have a blurry memory of bellowing, "This, man, this, we, okay, we chose this mess. Why? Why?"

Upon hearing that a relative had announced his vote for Trump and urged national unity post-election, I yelled, "FUUUUUUUUUUCK THAT GUUUUUUYYY."

My sister-in-law usually shuts me down when I swear in front of my seven-year-old niece, but she didn't, or wasn't able to, this time.

December 5, 2016

I left one of the burners on overnight. Somehow, I didn't start a fire. The smoke detector didn't even go off. I went in the kitchen in the morning to make coffee and saw that it was on.

But I have this feeling that there are all these burners around the world that are on and forgotten and there will be nobody to turn them off before everything is aflame.

December 10, 2016
I wanted to put an anti-Trump message in Christmas lights in our living room window, the one that faces the house that had that Trump/Pence sign last fall. But R. was worried about somebody breaking the window with a rock and the cats getting out via the broken window.

December 14, 2016
R.'s kid tells me that, in his high school, some kids are chanting TRUMP TRUMP TRUMP in the halls, and there are fist fights between Trump and HRC supporters in the restrooms.

December 20, 2016
A co-worker told me of how a guy called her a Mexican bitch after she beat him to a gas pump. Immediately before, while waiting to use the gas pump, she'd been reading this article addressing the question as to whether we live in post-racial times.

December 23, 2016
I'm going to D.C. to the Women's March with R., and I'm excited about my sign. R. found a round piece of cardboard that is close to the diameter of my rear wheelchair wheels. I found twine and will use that to secure the cardboard to the wheel spokes, making a wheelchair hubcap. Riffing off the idea of the vagina dentata that is associated with Athena's aegis, I drew on the cardboard an abstract representation of a vagina lined with teeth and printed

VAGINA DENTATA across the sign so that people would get it.

To obtain paint for my vagina, I called up the one arts-and-crafts person I know, R.'s ex-wife. She wasn't familiar with the phrase *vagina dentata*, so I explained and asked if she had particular colors of paint. We don't have the kind of relationship where the pinkness of labia is a regular conversation topic. So, I got flustered to the point where I forgot her fiancée's name. I asked if she could ask "her guy" to bring me the vagina paint from her house and got off the phone in a hurry.

January 5, 2017

@therealDonaldTrump blocked me on Twitter. I reported this to R., and he looked alarmed. But all I've done is retweeted political news from a handful of mainstream sources and tagged my posts with hashtags that are anti-Trump in some way. But the hashtags have been things like #women's march, not #armed revolution.

January 21, 2017

Women's March. In Arlington, R. and I got to the Metro and spent an hour on the platform and then maybe two hours on the train to travel the three stops between Crystal City and the Mall.

When we got off the train at L'Enfant Plaza, every inch of the station was crammed with people. The escalators weren't moving. The elevator was broken. R. and I waited, along with other people in wheelchairs and on crutches or walkers, for the elevator to be fixed. After a half-hour that brought the total time underground to around three hours, I sort of freaked out and declared that I was going to get out by pulling myself up the stairs with my freakishly strong arms.

I prepared to lurch out of my chair onto the stationary escalator stairs; R got ready to fold up the chair so he could carry it up behind me.

But then, one brave soul said he could lift my chair from the left, R. got the right, and somebody supported me from the back, and thus I was borne up the stairs. The chants of THANK YOU THANK YOU THANK YOU rang out from the hundreds of people around us on the stairs and people in the long line waiting to get on the stairs. I felt like a football on its way to the end zone.

I thought that my sign would be unique, and while I spotted no other wheelchair hubcaps, there were a few other vagina dentata manifestations. Two women had vagina dentata baseball caps, with toothy vagina felt sculptures on the brims. Several people took pictures of my vagina dentata wheelchair hubcap, asking me to roll forward or backward so that the words vagina dentata were level.

There were many representations of uteri in the signage, but only one penis sign that I saw. It was an erect penis, maybe three feet long, complete with painted veins and pubes. I guess that if you wanted a sign that would stand out at a women's march, a three-foot erect penis would do it.

February 10, 2017
I've been thinking about the idea that the election results were based on anxiety, economic anxiety, racial anxiety.

I'm in a heightened state of anxiety because I broke my leg, specifically, my tibia near my knee, when fell out of my chair. It took me two days to go to the hospital because I couldn't feel the break, so I didn't know what was going on. It wasn't until my leg swelled and turned red that I got to the ER, where there was talk about blood clots and infection.

Although now I'm on antibiotics and the doctors think no blood clots are involved, a CAT scan revealed significant bone loss, which often occurs with spinal cord injuries. So, I'm at great risk of breaking something else if I fall again.

Prior to this development, I didn't fear falling out of my chair. I fall when I overbalance while petting a cat or if my chair hits a rough piece of asphalt at the wrong angle or for a hundred other reasons. If I'm outside, I need to wait for a kind and strong person to come along. If I fall at home, the cats are alarmed, but I use nearby furniture to get back into my chair with a few minutes of undignified struggle. I'd fallen so many times without injury, I'd started thinking of my lower half as being inviolable as well as insensate.

This anxiety that comes with the knowledge that my body is a lot more fragile than I thought makes me want to rewind to the time when I was blissfully ignorant. I miss not worrying about my bone density mass, the side effects of calcium supplements, and how I'm supposed to navigate that one crosswalk on my commute to work where the winter weather has worn away the asphalt.

I'd been warned by doctors years ago that life in a wheelchair would result in bone loss. Why did I think that I was somehow exempt from the effects of fifteen years' worth of physics and time? Why would I want to delude myself?

The experience has made me think of people who deny that climate change exists. The kids of the Trump/Pence voting people who live behind us are going to witness the effects of climate change, if the scientists are right. Their parents have a choice: their children face a perilous future or the scientists are lying. Why not vote for the person who assures them of the latter, more comfortable reality? If they can believe science is a lie, they can ignore existential threats.

And can I, who until recently viewed collisions with the ground as mere inconveniences and now will be wearing a full-length leg brace until May, judge them?

February 28, 2017
One of my students said that Trump was America's mirror. She also told me that she'd been called the N-word a bunch of times, in Philly, by white people. How, in light of her experience, do I argue that she's wrong about the mirror thing?

March 10, 2017
I can't stop watching Sean Spicer press conferences. It's like watching YouTube videos of self-inflicted destruction. Like that one where somebody put a brick into a washing machine and ran the machine with the brick in it, with bits of the machine flying off as the brick rattled frantically, destroying the machine from the inside out, until all that was left was a manically spinning cylinder.

Sean Spicer reminds me of that.

March 17, 2017

I made the mistake at a recent therapy session of bringing up Sylvia Plath. I did so because R., while knowing a crazy number of other things, revealed that he hadn't heard of Sylvia Plath until I mentioned her. I brought up Plath with my shrink only to illustrate R.'s weird lacunae of ignorance.

My psychiatrist asked a couple of probing questions about my affinity for Plath's work. I made the very tasteless joke that given the current political situation, I understood the appeal of taking a bunch of drugs and crawling under a house. He sat up, looking concerned.

I wonder if he has other patients who are despairing about the state of the nation. Maybe he is. At a session a few days after the election, I made another tasteless joke, this one about the peace of the grave, and my psychiatrist started laughing until he began coughing. He's in his late eighties and has memories of the Great Depression. I wonder what it's like to live through all that and have to deal with President Donald J. Trump in the last years of his life.

April 20, 2017

I feel like we're in this moment of the cartoon coyote pedaling furiously in the air after going off a cliff while chasing the roadrunner; we're poised above the abyss, and soon we'll look down and plummet, a little cloud of smoke marking our departure.

May 11, 2017
Something about Trump's taking the credit for creating the expression "priming the pump" strikes me as very weird and troubling. I know it's not threatening thermonuclear war, but it's still psycho.

June 4, 2017
Felt sick when Trump used the terrorist attack in London to make a non-sequitur about liberals and gun control. Every. Damn. Day. There is a new thing. It's a cumulative effect: if he'd just shut up for one minute, maybe I'd recover from, say, the withdrawal from the Paris Accords, but no.

I'm in a much darker place than I was when I was at the Women's March.

The Trump supporter who lives within view of my living room window had patriotic bunting and flags all over his house for Memorial Day; I wanted to tear down his flags and scream in his face: THESE ARE NOT FOR YOU.

I feel like I have a duty to not tune out current affairs, but, at the same time, I can see that constant exposure to this malignancy that's infecting the republic is not exactly a recipe for mental health.

June 11, 2017
I mentioned to my acupuncturist that I'd been grinding my teeth in my sleep, as per R. I suggested that it was politics-related stress. Then the acupuncturist and I talked about Donald Trump while she stuck me all over with needles.

June 17, 2017

Last night, R and I had a deeply uncomfortable discussion about where all of this is going. I told him the thing that's been scaring me the most recently is that I'd always assumed that the countdown to bad shit happening would take a while to run down. I'd assumed that the clock had started ticking on 11/9/16.

But what if it started earlier? What if it started under Clinton? Reagan? Before that?

June 20, 2017

I've been thinking about King Lear and Trump, and as per my Twitter feed, so are a lot of other people.

But I haven't been contemplating the figure of the Mad King so much. I've been thinking more about how Lear cuts your heart into pieces by restoring order for a second. And even when Cordelia and Lear are captured, he is sane, and they are reconciled. Of course, that moment is short-lived.

I was thinking this because I was fantasizing about some outcome via these various investigations that would restore order.

But one of the dark truths in Lear is that once the existing order is torn down, it can't be easily restored.

I had a Shakespeare professor who argued that there is no alleviation of the misery presented in that play. That when Lear and Cordelia are imprisoned like birds in a cage, and Lear consoles Cordelia with a vision of an immortal love, this moment is not one of transcendence. It is only the cruelty of a false hope, as not soon later, Lear's sanity leaves him again as he holds Cordelia's corpse and his grief stops his heart.

But what if that moment of clarity and love does continue to exist despite the darkness that succeeds it?

Can we use our dwindling supplies of hope to believe that America's humanist ideals, currently under siege, will outlive "packs and sects of great ones, / That ebb and flow by the moon" (Shakespeare 5.3.19-20)?

I think of that magnificent hawk of about a year ago, coasting, until it was felled by the heat, over the city that birthed the nation. It was returned to the skies by people who just wanted to do a good thing.

Is perhaps that moment, in some intangible way, more important than the meanness that followed it?

TAMPON TRIGGER

DIANA KIRK

Dear Facebook Commenter,

I read your words a few weeks ago on my page. Remember when you commented on my post about taxing tampons and pads and women's underwear? You said, "I'm so happy I don't have to listen to my ex-wife talk about her periods and leaky stuff anymore." I was like, oh my god, how horrible for this guy to have to hear about MY problems on MY Facebook after a divorce. Well, I'm writing you a private message today because I just keep thinking about you. A lot. I mean dang, I am so sorry I brought up Aunt Flow. It sounds like it was a trigger for you.

In fact, I thought about you yesterday when I was at this fancy work event in my 4-inch Louboutin heels and lipstick. I wore my expensive bra too, the one that keeps me from breathing but is so worth it because when work requires "fancy," it is time to bring those girls out! And I think a couple of your buddies were at this event.

Weren't they? Aren't Phil and Tom our mutual friends? Middle-aged, comb-overs; Phil looks like maybe too much scotch on weeknights; Tom kinda looks 30-weeks prego with twins. No? You sure? I swear that's why I agreed to Friend you last year after that convention in Las Vegas where young ladies were giving out free body shots as a promotion for Prospect Mortgage.

Anyway, I thought about you at this work thingy because your buddies, Tom and Phil, were knee-deep in conversation when I tried to hand them my business card while also micro-hemorrhaging. We were all standing next to the latte machine. That's what they were serving at this meet and greet. Lattes and bagels with smears. I never got a bagel because I had to keep running to the ladies' room to change my plug. I was so worried about annoying Phil and Tom with a bloody crotch that I ended up just leaving early because I had run out of super-plus-plus tampons and my pantyliner was soaked. I mean, I should have known. It was my second day and as most period experts know, that's hemorrhage day. When us ladies do what you do at work while attempting to catch a quart of blood onto a thumb size piece of cotton shoved deep into our cavernous vaginas. I mean what would happen if I leaked? Poor Phil and Tom didn't need to see any of that. Plus, they seemed pretty busy talking about really important stuff like this week's news about AICs 80% investment portfolio at 6.5%. They weren't in need of stupid distractions like my hemorrhaging.

And when I got home from work, I thought about you again when I sat on the toilet because blood and clots were pouring out of my lady bits. Just oozing out. Like, you could hear them plopping into the toilet. Of course, right after that happened, I blacked out and hit my head on the tiled wall next to me. Oops. But, let me tell you, that doesn't happen very often these days because whew, can I get a hallelujah for progesterone patches? Right?

I'm just saying, I totally get it. How annoying would that have been to find your wife laying on the bathroom floor bleeding out of her nether regions with walnut-sized clots hanging off her carefully trimmed pubes. Seriously, walnut-sized! To think she talked to you about that stuff. Ugh, what a hag.

And then last night, again, I felt so bad for you and, really, guys in general. Here it was, the middle of the night and my poor husband had to sleep next to me while I night-sweated and bled all over our mattress. I mean that's what you're talking about, right? My poor husband's sleep could've been disturbed as I kept getting up to change my blood-soaked clothes and harpoon throughout the night. That poor, poor man!

So here I am today at work, a little bit woozy and definitely in need of a steak but concerned that I might have upset you a couple of weeks ago. I think I was insensitive to your needs, and I bet other men could relate to how awful it is to listen to all of our whining about migraines and cramps and chocolate. I mean, really, who needs to hangout with an anemic space alien? I know the answer. . . nobody. Right?

I feel as though I should thank you today. Now that I can see all of this clearer from your insightful comment on my post. So, on behalf of your ex-wife and women in general, thank you, for putting up with all of this menstrual/estrogen/progesterone bleeding cooter talk women overshare with men folk. I'm sure it's been a difficult time and I personally wouldn't want to make things more complicated for you. So thanks for stopping by my Facebook post and showing your support. The male perspective is invaluable to how I, as a woman, should live my life day-to-day. Sorry again for triggering awful memories with my tampon talk.

I'M THAT CHICK WHO STARTS THE CONVERSATION

RHONDA JACKSON JOSEPH

I'm that chick. The one that's used to being one of a few, if not the only, black woman in certain settings. Like going to horror conferences and only laying eyes on maybe two other black women, at most. Or like being the only black person within hundreds of miles of the small Transylvanian town that hosts an annual vampire film and arts festival, where Vlad Tepes was born. The one whose skin is unapologetically dark, whose hair changes with her moods. The one who constantly has to fight to represent black women in horror centered academic circles.

When I walk into my classrooms, I'm used to the myriad of looks. Some students wonder why my hair is so big. Others wonder why I speak so loud that they can hear me just fine in the back. Yet others are bored and rue the day they decided to go to college, only to be told they had to take at least one composition class for their certificate or degree. A smaller number is in awe: *my professor is a black woman.*

When I explain that my MFA is in creative writing and that I write horror fiction, I can win over some skeptics. Some students furtively check Google to verify my "outlandish" claims. Others wonder how a middle aged, urban, kind of suburban, round and fluffy lady writes horror. Yet others wonder why I'd even want to write that stuff. Very few are impressed: *my professor is a black lady who writes horror fiction.*

I've heard all the admonishments. My Southern Baptist upbringing didn't allow for little black girls who wanted to out the monsters on paper, especially those who also wanted to be the monster sometimes. It was okay to announce that I'd be a writer, even if it was romance fiction, because that was okay for ladies to do. I hid my horror writing persona high up in a big, tall tree, where I could peek and see her but where others wouldn't care to look. I fed her all the horror I could find. We visited all the time. I loved on her and she nourished my spirit. But we couldn't love each other publicly. I always prodded her back into the tree, so we both could remain safe. They weren't ready for us.

I wasn't ready for us.

I'm that chick who took her old black ass to graduate school and had to scour the town for a can of oil sheen when I left mine back home. The town's Walmart had one little, four-foot shelf of ethnic hair products. I took the tiny can of oil sheen they offered. Coconut and olive oil in a pinch weren't yet a thing. Hair products were scarce, and other beauty services for black women were pretty much non-existent. I'm not sure the town was ready for my blackness, but Seton Hill

University seemed to be. In that predominately white space, I found a welcoming group of horror writers who changed my life.

"Are you sure you're a romance writer?"

"You have a great dark side." No pun intended.

"You're really one of us."

I went in a romance writer and came out a better writer, period. And those kind and genuine souls gave me a ladder to help my horror girl down out of the tree. I could love her in full view of the world. We could do all the things that people in love did. She was so happy to be free! I was ecstatic I could treat her the way she deserved to be treated. When I was able to do that, she and I became the indomitable chick we are now.

It's hard as hell writing horror in a still male dominated space, especially one that will tell you it seeks diversity but doesn't really. It can only happen on its own terms, with severe limits. Frustrating isn't the word for getting rejections saying your characters aren't realistic, where you have to face the fact that they weren't deemed realistic only because they didn't conform to the palatable stereotypes that get recycled over and over again. Equally debilitating are the acceptances where you want to believe that your work was good enough for the gatekeepers but you have a hard time quieting the little voice that tells you your story only met their diversity quota. People look you straight in the face and tell you that black folks don't read, write, or watch horror. You wonder where that leaves you.

Horror gatekeepers announce in open forums that horror fans only want certain types of stories and characters. You wonder how that can be proven if the fans are only given that type of story and character over and over again. How will they know if my blackity black horror could be what they want if The Powers That Be never serve it up? How does anyone know they aren't craving true diversity and yearn for my stories, told about people who look like me, from my experiences? What about all the other stories that can come from other experiences? What about all of us?

I'm that fed up chick. The one who writes anyway. The one who understands that my work will never be enough for anyone but me. I'll probably have to always provide my own accolades. The one who doesn't know how to not write. The one who wants to escape back into the tree with my horror writing girl, and take our love back behind closed doors, but who is halted by the positioning of the ladder. It doesn't go up into our tree now. It goes across, to take us to the other side.

When I start a presentation on black femininity and the horror genre, I know what's coming. Some audience members wonder why I have to pull the black card. Others are angry they chose my talk—black women in their horror genre, indeed!—and scan the program for somewhere else to go. Yet others squirm uncomfortably, wanting to listen but not wanting the discomfort or self-imposed guilt. Just enough are excited: *we're ready for this discourse and we're totally here for progress.*

I'm that chick who starts the conversation.

MAXIMUM INSECURITY DICK PRISON

KIM VODICKA

I'll always remember the orgasms of my late teens and early 20's because I couldn't feel them.

They say it's not the destination that counts, but the journey. They say this about sex, too—that the orgasm is but one small component of a much vaster human experience—as though to strive for the climax somehow cheapens the fucking.

Whoever who first said this doubtlessly had a penis.

The orgasm gap is a real thing. It's at the bar every night. It's telling you, "The pleasure's all mine."

That's not to say I found no enjoyment whatsoever in the sex I had during my questionably spent youth. I just never knew how to demand my own maximum pleasure. I never understood how to insist upon my own supreme ecstasy in a society that routinely meets female sexuality with abject horror, censorship, crucifixion, exile, and, needless to say (though it keeps needing to be said), systematic oppression.

I started out as scared of sex as I was absolutely obsessed by it. I was as scared of sex as I was scared to admit it. It filled me with incapacitating anxiety. I self-medicated by getting incapacitated before fucking, and while I'm being painfully honest, I'll admit that the preponderance of the sex I've had in my lifetime has been drunk sex, which has rarely, if ever, been climatic.

Self-mutilation tends to take on different forms as we age. I was a cutter in my teens, but as I moved into adulthood, my self-harm practices transmogrified into a pathetic concoction of regular binge drunkenness and unsatisfying sex. I got alcohol poisoning. I got the DTs. I got date raped. I dated abusive assholes. I fucked man-boys who didn't know how to use their dicks. I picked up diseases in cases where the sex was far from worth it. I was killing myself, but in a more socially acceptable, young-girl-just-trying-to-find-herself fashion. I got fucked up and jumped on dicks in an attempt to feel less dead inside, as I deadened and deadened quick.

After coming to an awareness of this pattern, in my mid-20's, I experienced a years-long sexual-existential breakdown. I fucked maybe three times in as many years. Any attempt to discuss my need for gratification with my then-partner, a self-proclaimed "feminist" man, was met with resistance, hostility, and occasionally full-tilt temper tantrums. I found myself tip-toeing around his fragile masculinity. My desires apparently threatened his prowess.

The orgasm gap is a real thing. It sleeps beside you every night. It acts like you're the problem if you don't cum when it fucks you. It says, "Goodnight," before it rolls over and farts.

I'd fucked at least 60 men in my lifetime up to that point, and I'd climaxed with maybe five of them altogether. This revelation nearly ruined me. As a self-proclaimed "feminist" myself, I felt like a failure. I felt guilty. I felt suicidal. I sank into the tar pit. I wanted to fill my vagina with cement. I wanted to douse it with gasoline, set it ablaze. I wanted to kill myself from the inside-of-my-pussy-out.

To be able to cum, I have to be on top. I have to be able to grind a consistently rock-hard cock for about 15-20 minutes in order for my pussy to explode. Sucking on my titties, squeezing them together and sucking on both nipples at the same time, expedites the process, as does spreading my ass cheeks and fingering my butthole. Talking dirty is also a plus—the filthier, the better. I like age play. I like BDSM. I have a slobber fetish. I have a piss fetish. I like to play with cum. I'm also polyamorous. You need to be down with that.

Is that too much to ask?

Fuck. No.

I left my then-partner around the time I turned 28. I quit drinking for about a year. I got off of hormonal birth control (from which my body and mind narrowly dodged collapse). I moved to another state. I grabbed my life by the cunt. I took my cunt into my own hands and almost immediately started getting what I wanted—at first, with the help of an old flame's patience, not to mention his enormous penis, and after that, via a compassionate yet virile lover so committed to making me cum every single time we fucked that he often sacrificed his own orgasms.

It's always irritating when trite expressions wind up being true, but communication really is crucial to having great sex. Now that I know how to communicate what I want, and how to do so unabashedly, I've gone on to have consistently gratifying sex. I will never fuck again without advance knowledge that the person is not only willing, but enthusiastic, about giving me what I want. The person also needs to be cool with a hairy pussy because I'm never shaving that shit ever again. Though I wish my story were unique, it isn't. A man, upon sticking his dick in any given hole, is almost guaranteed to cum. The same is not true for a woman. There are women who have still never felt the thrill of orgasm, women whose pussies have never had the opportunity to explode, whose orgasms would kill you if you felt them. We absolutely must insist upon our maximum pleasure in order to get what we want, and we must permit ourselves to do so brazenly and intrepidly.

Sexually Powerful Women—remember that we are made of special metals. It is not possible for us to weaken. Be a bitch. Be a slut. Be a cunt. Be about it. Wear your badges of nastiness like a fucking Life Scout. Do whatever it takes to get off. Look your beast deep in the fucker. Whether you enjoy one man at a time or suck eight dicks at once, be proud of that. Respect yourself for that. Masturbate to that. Use a vibrator, an electric toothbrush, a hot tub jet, a garden hose, the edge of the bed. Use the world around you for your pleasure. Use the male anatomy to your advantage. Have sex so good, it may as well be a disaster movie. Let the rage of the wounded feminine lift you.

Fuck fucked up fuckers who make you feel fucked up about fucking.

Go fuck yourself.
Get fucked.
Fuck everyone.

YOU'RE SO NASTY
BOODAWE

I used to hear that a lot when I was a teenage punk girl in Los Angeles. It was the '80s, so calling girls like me "Nasty" or "Slutty" came with being in "the scene." I wasn't nasty when I was 13, or even 14—I mean not *REALLY* nasty—I just wore really short skirts with ripped up tights and fishnets. Shirts with cut-off sleeves so deep you could see my bra and waist. But I didn't see that as provocative— more rebellious if anything. At 15, something inside me changed. I lost my virginity at 14, but was all stupid and in love, then I got dumped and swore of sex for a year.

At 15, I felt this surge of power within. I was taught my place as an indigenous woman after getting my first moon. That women are life givers, and that we are to be honored for that gift. I never thought of myself in that light before, it was so empowering. I felt strong and special. My sexuality came rushing through me like venom. I kissed boys and yearned for more. I kissed girls and yearned for even more. But girls my age were much more reserved, and my desire to taste them remained unfulfilled.

I began finding myself in the dark corners of the clubs I attended, like a vampire waiting to feed. I was waiting for that one person I would choose to lure into my world, sneak into my bedroom for a night. I was good at this. Seducing guys to spend the night with me was very easy. Trying to let me dominate them and make them feel uncomfortable with my requests? Not so much. Asking someone to choke me was the one thing that would stop a guy in a hot minute. A look of confusion apparent on their face as they asked if I was serious. A stern expression on my face as I told them that I absolutely was.

In my late teens/early '20s, I came out of the closet as bisexual and found myself realizing that I didn't want relationships, just dates. I was too insatiable to be with one person as I knew I would eventually cheat, and I wasn't comfortable with polyamory. So I was just a self-proclaimed slut, and I remained as such into my '30's. I had sex with women in bar bathrooms, cars, and even on sofas in the apartment of a friend of a friend. I dated several women at one time and felt so surprised at my ability to woo women I felt so enamored with. Each date was different. Every sexual encounter, different. I thrived sexually and began to feel more comfortable in my body.

I remember this one time I was visiting this girl up in Northern California. She was a well-known Riot Grrrl and really involved in zine culture. We had sex on a hot summer day. We wore slips and ripped fishnets. It was the kind of passionate sex you know can only happen once. I felt her all over my face and fingers and thighs for the rest of the day . . . it was incredible. When it was over, we laid in her bed smoking and looking at each other, knowing it was only going to be this one time. We remained friends for a few years, then drifted apart, as is the case with many lovers I've had.

As I explored my pulsing sexuality, I found myself not only wanting to dominate my sexual partners, but wanting to also be dominated. It wasn't until I moved to the east coast and met another woman of color who taught me how to top from the bottom, how to flog, use paddles and knife play. Flogging became my favorite past time. The sting and the smell of the leather, the bruises. It was so . . . intoxicating. Whenever I'd see bruises left behind by lovers, I felt happy. The bruises were like little secrets I'd keep safe. But most of my partners were not comfortable with hitting me during sex or engaging in the other types of fetishes I had, so I often had to look outside of my relationships for BDSM fixes. To this day, at 46, getting my ass kicked while getting fucked, is when I feel the most feminine, strong, and powerful. Knowing my body can feel pleasure and pain and give life, is one of the greatest honors I've been given.

I don't know where the desire of being hit, choked, as well as being happy when I see bruises from my lovers, came from. Maybe because I rarely felt anything growing up. Maybe because over the years as a teen, I became numb from being objectified and didn't feel connected to my body and didn't know how to use my voice. I do know that my journey is not unique and that my sexual prowess was something I gained from experimentation and meeting people that helped me open up about my desires. Having lovers that I trusted completely, allowing myself to be vulnerable and get what I want at the same time. Finding that balance in a BDSM relationship taught me how to be in control while being dominated and reinforced the cultural pieces of me and how everything and everyone is connected. We are taught that our life must be in balance, all aspects. Being able to tell a lover what I want while letting them feel as though they are in control, is what I found the most intoxicating. I can present as this "slutty" femme, but in all reality, I am the control freak who wants you to call me "Nasty."

THEY SAY SHE'S A SLUT

JESSIE LYNN MCMAINS

It was a sticky-hot night like any other night in the summer of 2005. I'd gotten off work and changed clothes in my car—swapped out my pizza stench-coated blouse and slacks for a vintage dress from the 1930s or 1950s—then headed to the bar I wasted most of my time at. As I sat there waiting for my friends to arrive, a girl walked up to me. I didn't recognize her, but she sure as hell knew who I was—the way she strode toward my table showed that she had a purpose, and not a friendly one. She sat down across from me without even asking if it was alright, pursed her glossy lips and glared at me for a few seconds, then said: "I've been wanting to talk to you."

"About what?" I asked.

"You slept with my boyfriend," she said.

•

Shit. I ran through a mental checklist of the boys I was currently seeing, or had recently slept with. I didn't think any of them had girlfriends, except maybe one—but he lived in New York City, so I felt pretty sure that she wasn't talking about him.

"Your boyfriend?"

"Well, my ex-boyfriend," she said. "This was two years ago."

No *wonder* I hadn't known which boy she meant. "Uh . . ."

"You do remember him, right? Punkbro Doucheweasel?" (Note: not his actual name.)

"*That* guy? Yeah, I remember him. What a jerk."

"Yeah, he is a jerk. That's why I broke up with him."

•

Her expression softened, and I thought for a minute that we might be able to bond over what an awful guy he was.

"Just so you know," I said, "I had no idea he had a girlfriend when I slept with him. In fact, as soon as I found out, I broke things off with him."

She didn't respond right away. I was about to offer to buy her a drink, a kind of alcoholic peace offering, when her brow furrowed and her mouth hardened into a thin line, again. Uh-oh.

"That doesn't fucking matter," she hissed.

She started talking about all the stories she'd heard about me—the rumors, the reputations—most of which were exaggerated versions of actual events. She ranted about girls like me, "the kind of girls that sleep with other people's boyfriends." She went on to call me all the familiar names: slut, bitch, cunt, whore. I'd heard them all, and many others, before. Hell, I wore most of those slurs as badges of honor. I'd raised myself on riot grrrl, had pictures of my idols and my peers adorning my walls; pictures where they had *SLUT, WHORE, WITCH*, and *BITCH* scrawled in lipstick or Sharpie on their chests, their bellies, their arms. Songs like "Rebel Girl" and "Teenage Whore" were my anthems. I'd been referring to myself as a slut since I was seventeen, when I told my first serious boyfriend that I needed to be able to fuck as many other boys and girls as I wanted, because I was horny all the time and one lover couldn't satisfy me. I'd been a sex worker on and off since I turned eighteen, so whore was just an honest job description. My bestie and I called each other cunt as a term of endearment. I sometimes sported a button that said *tramp*, and I liked to quote my favorite Queen Bitch, Lou Reed, and say: "Honey, I'm a cocksucker. What are you?"

•

But that night, those words stung. It's one thing to reclaim a slur for yourself, or to have your best friend use it in a joking way, but it's a much different thing to have someone use a word against you out of hatred. Her accusations got me thinking of my lovers. I was seeing and sleeping with a handful of people at that time, and most of them wanted me to choose. Choose them and get rid of all the rest, or at least choose one person to be monogamous with. They wanted me to pick one lover and stick with them 'til death (or whatever) do us part. I was trying so hard—to choose, to be the good girl they wanted me to be—and I was failing spectacularly. Maybe that girl was right? Maybe my shitty exes who thought my high libido and desire for multiple partners was abnormal, and called me a slut and a freak—maybe they were right, too?

She was quiet for a second. I hoped she'd worn herself out. I was about to tell her to fuck off, but before I got the chance, she said: "Next time, you better make sure a guy doesn't have a girlfriend before you go and sleep with him."

I slugged back the rest of my whiskey and Coke. She continued: "All the people you've slept with, I'm surprised you don't have some fuckin' disease." Then she got up and walked away, and I bellied up to the bar.

"Another whiskey and Coke?" the bartender asked.

"No," I said. "Give me a Jameson, double. Neat."

"Are you okay?"

"No."

•

I returned to my table, clutched my whiskey glass in shaking hands. I felt an anxiety attack coming on—the sweat, the dizziness, the fluttery, jittery heartbeat. I'd been tested for STIs several times, most recently a few months before that night, and I was pretty good about having safer sex. But that girl's anger, combined with the circumstances of my love life, made me think: "Maybe I *do* have some fuckin' disease." This was during a period of my life when I had anxiety attacks almost every day, and I had just finished reading a novel in which the main character had syphilis. I began to panic that I had syphilis—suddenly, my mosquito bites were marks of syphilis, and my anxiety and sadness were signs of impending insanity. It was an irrational fear, but panic disorder is not a rational thing.

I went to the clinic a week later, got tested for every possible STI. I did not have syphilis, or anything else, but my encounter with that girl stuck with me. For years, whenever I had the kind of relationship problems that involved me wanting to be polyamorous and my partner getting upset about that, on sad nights when I lay around and wondered what was wrong with me, I thought of that girl. I pictured her furrowed brow and pursed lips, remembered her revulsion and the way she'd turned the words I'd once claimed with pride into weapons.

•

It took me nearly a decade, but I came back around to realizing that there isn't anything wrong with me. There's nothing wrong with me wanting to fuck boys, girls, and non-binary babes, or wanting to date more than one person at a time. There's nothing wrong with me whether I have a high libido or a low one. If I want, I can get gang banged every day for a week straight, then not have sex again for a year. As long as I'm honest and open about my desires, and everyone involved is consenting, it's all good.

Another thing that took me almost a decade was being able to forgive that girl. I'm no longer mad at her. Instead, I'm mad at the culture we live in. I'm mad at right-wing "abstinence only" sex education. We need to teach people the truth about all aspects of sex, including Sexually Transmitted Infections. Yes, they need to learn about safer sex and how to stem the spread of STIs, but we also need to destigmatize STIs. People need to know that contracting an STI is not a sign of being "dirty," or even promiscuous;

that you can contract an STI from having some form of sexual contact only once. And they need to know that promiscuity is not, in and of itself, a bad thing.

I'm mad at the patriarchal thinking that pits women against each other for the attention and affections of shitty men, and teaches us that it's not the man's fault if he strays beyond the boundaries of his relationship. It is that sort of mindset which made that girl so angry with me. Even though she'd since broken up with Punkbro Doucheweasel, and admitted he was a jerk, there was a part of her that couldn't believe the blame lay solely on his shoulders. So she had to find a scapegoat, and it was easy to paint me as the villain, the femme fatale who lured the poor innocent man into an affair. I wish we lived in a culture that held men responsible for their own actions. I wish we lived in a culture that taught girls to have each others backs, taught us to say: "Hos Before Bros."

I wish that the night she confronted me, I'd had the temerity to say: "Oh, girl. If he hadn't cheated with me, he would've done it with someone else." I wish I could find her now, tell her that her words hurt me but that I understand why she said those things. I wish I could find her and serenade her with "Rebel Girl," sing: *they say she's a slut, but I know*—I wish I could find her and say: "We should be best friends, not enemies. Now, can I buy you that drink?"

THE UNITED STATES OF RAPE CULTURE

KATHRYN LOUISE

The term 'rape culture' refers to our systematically rooted judgement toward rape victims and society's normalization of sexual violence. Think pieces on the topic circulate whenever a rape case makes national headlines but our conversations about rape culture are infrequent and lacking in substance.

We give men permission to tune out by referring to the topic as a "women's issue" when we should be making them a focus of the conversation[1]. We need to talk about why male victims are less likely to report and why men are so often perpetrators of sexual and physical violence against the feminine. We need to talk about white masculinity and the fact 57% of perpetrators of sexual violence are white[2].

---

[1] Jackson Katz has a wonderful TEDx Talk on this topic.
[2] RAINN (Rape, Abuse & Incest National Network) has more data on male victims and perpetrators. https://rainn.org

We must take time to consider those frequently left out of the discussion—rape is a human issue and affects everyone on the gender spectrum.

We need to stop treating sexual violence as an exceptional horror and must embrace it as a reality of everyday life. There are no isolated incidents.

We need to discuss the intersections of sexual violence and race, class, disability and sexuality.

We need to make more room for native women and femmes and acknowledge what it means they are at the highest risk for experiencing sexual violence.

We need to stop focusing solely on date rape drugs, dark alleys and college campuses and start conversations about how often sexual violence occurs at the home and in church.

Sexual violence is so normalized in this country we now have an alleged rapist and self-admitted sexual assaulter in the White House. We need to talk about that.

We need to stop equating sex trafficking with sex work because that shit is dangerous.

We need to talk about the fact survivors are ten times more likely to use hard drugs.

We need to acknowledge rape is about power, not sex.

We need to talk about the ways in which we all uphold rape culture.

NUMBERS, NUMBERS, NUMBERS

Here in the United States, women aged 12-34 are at the highest risk of rape and sexual assault. I am currently 26 years old. I have been raped by two men and sexually assaulted by four others. I wonder how many more times it will happen over the next eight years.

I was under ten the first time it happened. My brother was two years older than me. Young, but old enough to know what he was doing when he invited me to play a game of doctor. I buried the memory for years, convinced myself it was a terrible nightmare born of a disturbed mind. Though my brother had always been violent, I didn't think him capable of *that*. I didn't even know what *that* was, I just knew I felt a sense of shame whenever I thought about it, so I let myself forget.

At 14 I was violently raped by a stranger. I will carry a piece of him with me forever, stored in my spine.

Between the ages of 14 and 16 I was routinely physically and sexually assaulted by a partner who coerced me into having non-consensual sex with other women, and once allowed some of his older male friends to sexually assault me while I was blackout drunk.

At 20, a friend proceeded to initiate sex with me despite the fact I couldn't stop laughing uncomfortably while we were undressing, and lay prone during. I struggle to think of this as rape because I had verbally implied consent before undressing and hadn't been able to say "no" during. At the least, I consider it an example of how traumatic sex can be if consent by both parties isn't clear and enthusiastic.

At 24, a photographer sexually assaulted me during a shoot. I didn't bother reporting it to police because I knew it'd only be a waste of time.

I wish I could say stories like mine were exceptional.

The truth is people like me are raped all the time.

An American is sexually assaulted every 98 seconds and 321,000 Americans are raped or sexually assaulted each year. Of those, 90% of adult victims and 82% of juvenile victims are female. 15% of rape victims are under the age of 12 and 34% of perpetrators in child sexual abuse cases are family members. Bisexual women have a 46.1% chance of being forcibly raped and a 74.9% chance of being coercively raped or sexually assaulted. 11.2% of college students experience rape or sexual assault[3].

I wonder what's been the leading factor for me—my gender, age, or sexuality. I no longer believe it's just my luck, though I did for a long time. When you've been the victim of multiple instances of sexual violence, you start to believe you invite it.

CONSIDER HOW WE TALK TO SURVIVORS

"How were you dressed?" "Can you prove it?" "I don't believe you." "You shouldn't be talking to me about this." "You were kind of asking for it." "How could you forget?!" "He probably didn't know what he was doing was rape." "He never did that to me." "Why would you laugh?" "You shouldn't talk about this—he's been through enough." "Are you sure that's what happened?" "That doesn't sound so bad. . ." "Didn't you make porn once?" "Don't you pose nude?" "Didn't you cheat on him?" "Didn't he pay you?" "He wouldn't do that." "I don't think that counts." "Why didn't you report it?" "Why were you out so late?" "Why were you there alone?" "Why didn't you fight back?" "Why didn't you ask for a rape kit?" "You're only speaking up now for attention." "You hate men." "You're just making a fuss." "Go to the Middle East—*that's* a rape culture!"

---

[3] These numbers (and more) can be found on the RAINN's website.

"I'd still fuck you." "What? So you want all men sent to jail with no due process?" "But what about all the false reports?""What about female perpetrators?" "You're a cunt." "Did it feel good?" "Do you like rape role-play?" "Would you recreate the experience for a custom video?" "You're tainted." "He tried to do that with me but I fought back." "Why does this happen to every girl I date?" "Can we change the topic?" "You're bumming me out." "Lighten up." "Not all men." "Yeah, but were there any witnesses?" "Does that *really* count as rape?" "If you report this, you could ruin his life." "Weren't you dating at the time?" "Did you scream or call for help? Why not?" "You talk about this too much." "Rape is a women's issue." "You're just trying to spread fear." "You probably deserved it." "You don't look like a rape victim." "Why aren't you talking about male survivors?" "There is no rape culture."

Those are some of the responses I've heard after sharing my story. I've kept track of them over the years because they remind me why I talk about sexual violence.

Not that I need a reminder. I can't stop thinking about sexual violence.

I think about it when I look in the mirror, where I see my brother's features in my own. I think about it when I look at my nephew's faces and see my brother's in theirs, wondering whether he's done the same to them and knowing the odds. I think about it walking to the grocery store, when I pass by my rapist on the street and wonder if he knows exactly where I live. I think about it on those rare occasions in which my mother discusses her own experiences with sexual violence. I think about it when I talk to my female friends and acquaintances. I think about it when I talk to my sister and wonder when or if I'll ever have a similar conversation with my other sisters. I think about it whenever I'm alone in public and approached by a man I do not know. I think about it when I lock my doors at night. I think about it whenever I have an outbreak of genital herpes. I think about it in the mornings when I take my medication. I think about it at work, whenever I pose for a male photographer I haven't met. I think about it when I check social media. I think about it when the bar downstairs plays "Blurred Lines." I think about it when I read the work of my male peers. I think about it when I see the anti-choice protesters outside Planned Parenthood. I think about it when I watch the news. I can't escape it in television, cinema, or literature. I can't even keep the topic out of my own fiction.

I think about it when I see pictures or hear the name of Donald Trump.

Here is a man who has admitted to sexually assaulting women. A man who later dismissed his admittance as "locker room talk." A man approximately 24 women have accused of sexual assault or actual or attempted rape[4].

A man we elected president.

We knew of at least two prior court cases before we elected him. Months before the 2005 *Access Hollywood* tape was released, we learned of a new allegation from a woman who claimed Trump raped her when she was 13 years old[5].

We still voted for him, though.

Of course we can't say for sure how many Trump voters

---

[4]See "Trump And The Truth: The Sexual Assault Allegations" by Jia Tolentino.
[5]See "Why The New Child Rape Case Filed Against Donald Trump Should Not Be Ignored" by Lisa Bloom.

knew his history of sexual violence before they voted for him, but an ABC poll states 68% of registered voters believe he has sexually assaulted women.

That didn't stop them from voting for him, though.

The election of Trump alone proves we live in a society that normalizes, forgives, and accepts sexual violence.

Judgement toward rape victims is systematically rooted in our government. Consider what it means that the new MacArthur-Meadows amendment of the American Health Care Act gives states the power to waive the ban on denying coverage for pre-existing conditions, the list of which now includes both sexual assault and domestic violence[6]. For many survivors it must feel like confirmation society considers them damaged beyond repair. It certainly won't motivate survivors to come forward.

ON SILENCE

My mom reported my rape to police. From my understanding they never bothered to file a report. I had no rape kit[7]. I could not give them the name of my attacker. I wasn't able to give them a good physical description. They seemed to doubt my narrative and told my mom there wasn't much they could do. The experience was damaging enough to keep me silent when my partner began abusing me. Now that I'm a little older and a little wiser I understand the fact my mom felt comfortable calling the cops either

---

[6]See "Health 'Reform' Will Make Sexual Assault Survivors Sick" by Gina Scaramella.
[7]The average cost of one is $1,000 - $1,500 and the United States has a serious backlog. www.endthebacklog.org has more info on this.

only goes to show our privilege or her ignorance at the scope of the problem. Calling the police simply isn't an option for everyone, and we all need to stop pretending it's our duty to push survivors into reporting.

Why bother speaking up when you know people won't believe you? 97% of perpetrators never face jail time and the occasional national media coverage sexual violence receives only serves to remind how light sentencing for this crime tends to be.

When I think of men like Donald Trump and Brock Turner I think how easy it is for wealthy white men to get away with rape. I think of the fact marital rape wasn't illegal in all 50 states until 1993 and that three women are killed by current or former male partners each day[8]. These things are connected.

The threat of further violence silences survivors. The cost of a rape kit deters us from getting medical help when we need it. Social stigmas silence us. Our own ignorance can keep us silent—we have a horrible understanding of consent in this country and propagate myths that seek to discredit survivors. Limiting our discussions and media representations of sexual violence only serves to narrow our understanding of it. Some people do not know they've been assaulted until someone else validates their experience by calling it what it is.

It doesn't matter why survivors choose to remain silent—it's their choice to make.

Shouldn't we as a culture be more focused on rapists anyway?

---

[8]Data from the National Network to End Domestic Violence.

SO WHAT CAN WE DO?

We can start by admitting we have a problem. Feminists and so-called social justice warriors can't be the only ones leading the conversation. We need to stop limiting discussions of sexual violence to cliché images of college campuses, dark alleyways, and stolen white female virtue and focus more on those we've been leaving out of the conversation. While we should continue to discuss the role men play in perpetrating sexual violence we cannot let ourselves forget the fact that male survivors are even less likely to come forward. Sexual violence affects everyone on the gender spectrum, not just women. We need to discuss the intersections of sexual violence and race, class, disability, and sexuality. We must acknowledge the fact that rape is about power, not sex, and that we are all responsible for upholding rape culture.

These will not be easy conversations but those worth having rarely are. If we do not break our collective silence, we will be lost in it, hurting both ourselves and everyone else.

I DIDN'T ASK FOR THIS

ELEANOR ROSE

When I tell people I'm a nude model, the first question I'm always asked (if they don't immediately decide I'm disgusting) is, "Is that safe?" Though no one ever actually says it, we all know the question actually means, "Won't you get raped?"

I usually talk about statistics and aim to reassure them: That though the freelance modeling industry is infamous for sex slavery and assault, the rates of this are, relatively, actually very low. That these atrocities are better combated through education than through telling people not to model. That the risks are largest for new models, and that they can be mitigated and almost entirely removed through research and care. That setting up a bio properly can establish you as an experienced professional who wouldn't make easy prey.

I talk about the fact that I faced far more regular sexual harassment working in a hospital and at a law firm than I have as a nude model.

What I don't say is that their innocent question is part of why the industry can be dangerous. I don't mention that when people decide that freelance modeling is a predator's paradise and that the women involved are putting themselves at risk, they're legitimizing the predators as just a natural part of the industry. I don't tell them how risky it is for nude models to speak up about this or the stigmas we'll face if we do. Nor do I tell them that if we do get assaulted or raped, we have far less of a chance of ever seeing justice done—which is saying something, since most rape kits are never processed and most rapists never even face a court, let alone time in prison.

I don't talk about being sexually assaulted multiple times, by multiple people, from the time I was six, because to do so would mean fueling the agendas of people who believe I must pose nude because I'm "damaged goods." I rarely mention that I was sexually assaulted four times on a college campus within two years, yet only twice as a model within the past six. Even though I'm far safer as a model than as a student, too many people will use those facts to justify their idea that I'm working in an unsafe field.

I rarely tell people that my journey as a model helped me learn to set boundaries and stay safe, because they latch onto the fact that there are dangers in this industry and dismiss any positive aspect I might be trying to share, ignoring the truth that the same dangers exist in for women everywhere within our culture, within our world.

I don't tell people that the day my father proudly announced he had figured out why I pose nude was the day I was told I'd been molested by a police officer as a child.

I don't talk about having to choose between speaking up about the issues I face as a woman or protecting myself and my peers from further stigma as a nude model.

But it's all true.

I do face a chance of sexual assault as a nude model. But before you assume that means I should change careers or am 'asking for it,' please understand that I face a chance of sexual assault as a woman, period. Nude modeling hasn't changed that, it just means I'm under even further pressure to stay quiet about it.

Out of all my friends and peers that I am close enough with to talk to about the subject, I don't know a single person designated female at birth who hasn't been sexually harassed. Many of those friends have also been assaulted at least once, often before they turned eighteen, and most of them haven't spoken up or pressed charges. There's little incentive to speak up when claims are so often ridiculed and dismissed—sexual harassment as 'just the way men are,' and assault as 'not that bad'.

The teacher's assistant only towered over me, grabbing my thigh as he lectured me, and refused to let go—why did I make such a fuss? It took me years to accept the fact that it's ok, and in fact accurate, to call that experience assault. But I'm urged not to make a big deal about it. The word assault can ruin someone's life—why would I throw it around and call wolf when all he did was touch my thigh? He didn't bruise me, he didn't grab my breasts . . .

But when someone else grabbed my breasts in class, I was warned by campus police that there was a low chance of the complaint going anywhere because while his actions 'weren't that big a deal,' it would 'seriously impact his education' if the charges stuck. We are taught from the time we are little girls that men's reputations are more important than our health and safety.

Given this, why is it surprising that I didn't say anything when a photographer I was shooting Shibari with grabbed my boobs while I was tied up (then later told me he thought it was okay because we were friends)? I reasoned that it might have just been a misunderstanding, and saying something could ruin his career, even though my health and safety was on the line.

I knew that if I spoke up people would say it was my fault because I was naked, because I let him tie me up. They'd say it was an inherent risk of my job, that I accepted it when I chose to pose for him, that I was lucky he didn't do worse, that I should change careers if I have a problem with it. I'd be viewed as proof of every stigma nude models face—the girl who was sexually abused as a child and decided to pose nude "because" of it; the nude model who was sexually assaulted on the job and thus "proved" that we put ourselves at risk.

When a photographer grabbed my crotch and started rubbing my clit while I was lying down, unable to get away. When he continued after I yelled at him multiple times to stop, I convinced myself it was my fault. It wasn't, but I told myself that because it was the only way I knew to handle the situation safely. I was in Utah, and I was naked in his house. Who could I have turned to?

For a week after, he pestered me asking why I was upset. When I finally got mad and told him that what he'd done was beyond inappropriate, that he'd touched me without consent and ignored me when I said no and told him to stop, he started crying. He told me that he had thought I was just playing coy because I was "ashamed of saying yes." That in his experience, "women always say no when they mean yes." He tried to make me comfort him, tell him it was ok and apologize for being mad.

Though it was the context within which I met the perpetrators, neither of those scenarios were a case of me being at risk because I was working with photographers. When someone thinks that it's ok to grab a woman's breasts because she's his friend, or that a woman means yes when she yells no, they're not going to limit predatory habits to the models they shoot with.

I faced these same issues when I interned at a hospital as a fifteen year old and was asked by a patient to give him a handjob during his sponge bath. I faced them when I worked at a law firm at age seventeen and was leered at by male employees, when my computer got a virus and the IT guy teased me about watching porn, when he cornered me for conversations I wasn't comfortable with and paid me compliments that weren't appropriate. I faced them in school, in my hobbies, in my jobs, and in every facet of my life. And I always knew that if I spoke up I'd be ridiculed, mocked, examined, and declared a bully and a liar. I was taught that sexual harassment and assault were the woman's fault long before I became a nude model.

I'm not alone. I wasn't the outlier who became a nude model to handle the abuse in a way I could "understand." I can almost guarantee you that every woman you know has faced these same issues. Quite plainly, if sexual assault, harassment, and rape made every woman who dealt with them become a nude model or sex worker, the American economy would cease to function.

Two of my female family members have been raped. Several of my friends have been raped. I don't know a single person designated female at birth who hasn't faced sexual harassment at the very least. This is a pervasive issue in our society, and my career and my nakedness have nothing to do with it. Claiming that these issues are because of my chosen career is not only hurtful and wrong, it perpetuates the issue and encourages further crimes by punishing the victim rather than the perpetrator.

That is why nude modeling can be dangerous—because accounts of experiences are dismissed as 'she asked for it' and predators think they can get away with anything.

But it's also why this industry can be safer than most. The stigma we face has created solidarity among nude models, and when no one else will help us, we help ourselves and each other. We talk, we share our experiences, we help each other heal when needed, and we make sure that predators are labeled as such and pointed out to every new model that comes under our wings. In an industry that refuses to regulate itself, we stand as regulators. We are changing the way things work.

But we shouldn't have to do this alone. We shouldn't have to stay quiet about our experiences in order to shelter our peers from stigma. We shouldn't have to pass on names and stories quietly because speaking out publicly would mean gaining bad reputations as 'divas' and 'trouble makers.' And we shouldn't have to fight to make an industry that relies on the trust of young women acknowledge that the responsibility of minimizing the risk we take should be on them, not on us.

S L E A Z E B A L L
GAMES OR
HOW I GOT
BANNED FROM
M A T C H . C O M

AMBER FALLON

If the internet is a cesspool, the world of online dating is a dumpster filled with flaming diapers, liquefied lettuce, and rancid salmon. Not exactly the kind of thing most sane people would wade into willingly; but still, if you want to find love you have to put yourself out there, right? That's what they told me, anyway. So, I donned my hazmat suit and took the plunge.

I was kind of embarrassed in the beginning. I mean, I hadn't dated anyone in a really, really long time. After getting out of an abusive too-long-term relationship, and spending several months working on myself and figuring out what I wanted in life, I began to feel like it was finally time to find someone to share my life with. I had no idea where to begin, so when a commercial for match.

com interrupted my viewing of something silly on *Adult Swim*, it seemed like a good idea to join up and see what happened. Oh, how wrong I was.

Getting started was easy, even kind of fun: answering questions, filling out the profile, selecting a few pictures—I was actually enjoying myself! Within minutes, a ding and a little indicator in the corner of my screen told me I'd received my first message.

His name was something generic. Billy or Bobby or something. His introductory message was equally as generic.

"Hey."

A single word. Then he hit send. I've never done this before, so maybe that's how this worked? I responded in kind and was instantly met with a picture of his junk. Seriously?! Ugh. I reported him and deleted the message, wishing I had something akin to eye bleach. I wondered if he'd sent me that picture because he couldn't get anyone to look at his small, misshapen junk willingly. Bleh.

Minutes passed and I had another message. This guy didn't even bother with the preamble, just BOOM, hello Mr. Johnson. What in the actual fuck? I reported him, too. I was just about to deactivate my account in disgust, relegating myself to a life of loneliness and misery in the company of my cat, when another message beeped into my inbox. There were actual words in his message, and no mention of his genitals. Things were off to a good start. As I perused his introduction, I started to feel better about my future with the site. His name was Jason, he was two years older than I was and living in the same city. He was cute, he seemed funny, and he shared my sarcastic sense of humor. He had even quoted my favorite movie (which I had listed in my bio). Win!

I messaged him back and we started chatting. We talked for hours and I hardly noticed the time flying by. When I looked up, the sun was starting to peek through the windows. I dashed off to grab a few quick hours of sleep before work, giddy and elated, dreaming of meeting the mystery man on the other end of the message window.

Over the next few days, we talked A LOT. Eventually, I gave him my phone number so we could hear each other's voices. It was scary in a stomach-full-of-butterflies way. I hung up from that first phone call four hours later, halfway believing I was in love. Could it really be that easy? This was the first person I'd felt anything at all for outside of my ex in over a decade. My world was rosy and bright.

Then came the other shoe, dropping like a garbage truck off the Empire State Building. You knew that was coming, didn't you?

I woke up to a text message from Mr. Fantastic, sent only minutes after our phone call ended.

"You are wonderful. I have to meet you!"

I smiled, feeling the same way.

"Um, yeah!" I responded, "Coffee tomorrow night?"

He took a few hours to respond. I was starting to get nervous. I kept telling myself I was being silly, that it was early in the morning and maybe he was asleep or at work or in the shower. Still, I was worried. Maybe I had scared him off? Maybe he was just toying with me?

At last he responded.

"Sounds good. One thing though."

Uh oh.

"Yeah?"

"I just . . . I can't go into this unless I know you're in it, too. For real."

"Of course I am! I like you. I want to see you in person."

"The thing is, I can't put my heart on the line unless I know we'd be a match physically, too."

Wait, what?

"What do you mean?"

"It would be best for both of us if we just got the physical stuff out of the way first. That way we'd know if we were compatible or not right away."

I was starting to see where he was going, but I didn't want to believe it.

"Physical stuff?"

"Sex."

Oh. Fuck.

"Wait, so you want me to agree to sleep with you on a first date? Are you serious?"

"I just need to see if we're compatible before I get my heart broken."

A flurry of emotions were competing for attention in my brain. I was angry, for one thing. Hell, I was FURIOUS. Did he think I was some naïve little pixie who would fall for that bullshit line? Had he used it on someone else before? AUGH! I was also disgusted. That line seemed so carefully crafted to manipulate women. Of COURSE it wasn't about sex! It was about compatibility! He didn't want to get his widdle heart bwoken. *Right*. I was also hurt. I hadn't really felt like that in a long, long time—the dizzy anticipation of talking to someone you're attracted to; the silly daydreams, the lovesick thoughts and feelings. He had torn that away from me with some truly sleazeball behavior. Feeling used like that just fueled my anger. I was Jean Grey come Phoenix. I was Ares, Mars, Wrath, and every one of the Furies, all rolled into one. He was going to pay, alright.

I took a moment to calm down, mostly for the sake of preserving my cell phone in its current working condition.

"Ok." I replied. A devious smile spread across my lips. This was going to be great.

"Really?"

Oh yes, this was going to be good.

"Yeah, I mean, it makes sense. But first, I have something to tell you. . ."

"Ok, what?"

"Please don't be upset, but. . . I stole those pictures. I like younger guys and I just—I didn't expect to meet someone like you."

"Stole them from who?"

"My daughter."

I expected this to be the killing blow. My theft of his dream of scamming a naïve chick into free sex the way he'd stolen my dream of meeting a decent guy to watch horror movies and eat sushi with.

Without missing a fucking beat, he responds with, "Oh, if she's your daughter, you must be hot! I'm down for some MILF action!"

FUCKER! No. Nope. This would not stand.

"Oh, sorry, no. I'm not her mother. I'm her father."

BWAHAHAHAHA! My rage escaped in a flood of maniacal laughter. I patted myself on the back for coming up with such a perfect response so quickly. My phone was silent.

"Are you still there?" I texted.

Message undeliverable. Hah! Jerk.

Whatever. There were more fish in the cesspool sea. I'd just have to be more careful next time. . .

I logged in to match.com to update my profile, only to discover I'd been locked out. I tried to unlock my account and, in doing so, discovered an email informing me that they had banned me after receiving a report that I had falsified my "gender and/or identity." *Huh.*

I briefly wondered how match.com's admins would feel about that little exchange. Somehow I doubted that their takeaway would be the same as Jason's. While he was technically correct, he was also a fucking bucket-of-slime-predator who tried to manipulate me into having sex with him. I decided I didn't want to deal with it, but I did still want to find love. . . or at least someone to giggle over silly web comics with. And so, somewhat more guarded and a good deal more cynical, I took the plunge into OKCupid.

HERE'S TO YOU, MRS. ROBINSON

TARA DUBLIN

I'm 48, and the last guy I fucked is 28.

Yeah, I still got it.

(Hey, hey, hey)

Before you drop that other C word that I hate, please know I don't do this on purpose. I'm not out every night in bars wearing low-cut tops and ill-fitting leather pants, preying on the Youngs. I don't use them to stave off real intimacy with someone closer to my age. I'm not seeking constant validation that I "don't look my age." It just kind of keeps happening to me, even though I'm never deliberately seeking it.

Of course, it's incredibly flattering to have a hot, young guy think I'm sexy—even if I'm technically old enough to have given birth to him. The millennial mindset toward age, sex, and basically everything else seems to be, "Whatever, bruh, let's just chill and see what happens."

Younger guys are certainly more energetic than middle-aged men, can have sex three and more times a night, and most likely never have had a truly proper blowjob. The 20-something girls may have less cellulite and no kids, but I have more experience. And I promise you, that's what makes the difference. Of course, younger guys also don't want to get into serious relationships, because they're still figuring stuff out, as they should be. And if they do want to get serious, it's because they want to get married and make babies, and I've already done that. My baby factory has been closed since 2003, my friends. I have one son in college and the other in high school. I've put in my time. So while they're fun and all, there comes a point where you have to decide what you truly want. But what I want doesn't seem to exist.

(We'd like to help you learn to help yourself)

I may be a confident and sexually potent woman in her prime, but I can't say that I'm good at any of this dating shit, because I'm not. I have two significant adult relationships under my belt. The first was with the father of my sons, J., aka The Wasband, whom I was married to for nearly ten years. That relationship blurred into the second one. As I was leaving my marriage, I met K., who remains the greatest love of my life up to this point. We were together six years, living together for most of it. Twelve and half years younger than I, K. was the one who showed me that I deserved to be loved and respected, and spoiled me for life. I never thought I'd be single again, but things change, and that's another story for another anthology.

So ANYWAY, in 2012 I found myself in new territory: single for the first time since college in the early 90s, when Nirvana was a cool new band and there was no such thing as internet dating. I learned that being a serial monogamist was the opposite of what was cool in Portland. Eventually I stopped dating like I was hunting for the last great love of my life, and started simply trying to enjoy myself. At the same time, I started working in the service industry, which is filled with a lot of cute, young, beardy guys who aren't shy about flirting. They will literally say anything as they test their budding flirting game. They love the idea of adding a Hot Older Woman to their Fuck-It List. What they aren't great at is following through, because they don't think they have to. You know from the outset they're not in it for the long-haul, because they essentially live consequence-free. I mentioned this fact to one of the cute Youngs I was working with at the time, who was all of 22 and had been hitting on me mercilessly.

"I have no desire to be the Mrs. Robinson of Portland," I told him.

"Who's she, your slutty neighbor?" he replied.

"Hey, thanks for making my point for me," I said, walking away and vowing I'd never touch a guy whose age started with a 2.

(Every way you look at this, you lose)

Hot sex without any emotional attachment or obligations sounds great to a lot of people—basically all the single guys in Portland live by it. Polyamory is THE thing here right now. But I'm an anomaly—I only want one person at a time. This is apparently a crazy thing to want. I'm sure everywhere is terrible for women in their later 40s (or any age; however, when it starts with a 4, it's waaaaay more challenging), but it seems the dating pool in this town is more like a shallow puddle. It's bad enough that no one wants to make a commitment, because what if there's someone better just one swipe away? It also doesn't help that every other guy on Portland Tinder is standing in a river holding a fish. I'm an indoorsy Jersey Girl stuck in the outdoorsy Pacific Northwest. I don't consider it a date if it involves going to REI first.

Plus, the internet and texting have utterly ruined human communication for the rest of our history. People you were chatting with post-match will just disappear. Ghosting is the opposite of adulting, but what can you do? It's not like they're ever going to respond, if you can even find them. Now you can fuck around with literally zero accountability. I've been ghosted a couple of times, and it sucks so very much. Be a fucking grownup and tell a girl you've moved on. It's not that hard to say, "Hey, I enjoyed our time together, but it's not really working for me. Best of luck to you!"

My most recent experience with this particular phenomenon occurred with A. (not his real initial), who, at 31, was at the older end of the Youngs spectrum. A. local chef who had done very well on a nationally televised cooking competition, A. reached out to me via Twitter the night after the election to commiserate with my despair. He offered his listening services, "even in person," if I needed to talk. Though we had never met in person, I felt like I knew him thanks to the TV show (I'd also developed a small crush on him because he's adorable) and our social media friendship. I'd assigned him the qualities of maturity and kindness I'd seen during the season. Combined with the fact that he was the head chef of one of the best restaurants in town, I presumed he would handle himself like a responsible adult, since he had to command a line of cooks often older and definitely larger than he. And let's put a pin in that line of thinking for the moment.

While I fully realize that it was historically one of the worst possible times to make any kind of a life decision, I appreciated A.'s offer of a shoulder to wail on. We met at my house, because I didn't want to have my nervous breakdown in a bar. We sat at my kitchen table nursing the Stella Artois he'd brought, and he let me go and on while we took turns hitting my bong. At some point during my monologuing, I caught him looking at me in a very not-just-friends-like way, his blue eyes full of desire rather than sympathy. I'm so hot when I'm distraught, y'all.

"Did you come over here thinking you were going to hook up with me?" I asked, abruptly changing the subject from politics.

"Well," he replied with a half-shrug and a slight smile, reaching his hand out to take mine, "I've always thought you were super hot."

That sealed it. Turns out, I needed his shoulder to bite down on rather than cry on.

And thusly, we established ourselves as Friends With Benefits and no more. He is of the "someday wants to get married and make babies" faction, and that's fine. When we were together, he was indeed the sweet and kind guy I'd crushed on and rooted for. Like the Youngs before him, he was unprepared for the skill level of an experienced older woman. I could tell he was taken by surprise. I can't lie, there's something extraordinarily hot about knowing you're someone's best sex, even if they aren't yours. The fact that I'm often told I'm better at sex than most is one of those humblebrags you can't really share on Facebook, but it does put a little extra pop in your step the morning after.

However, despite being able to call orders to a busy line for hours on end, and despite telling me I gave him the best head he'd ever had, A. lacked the basic human communication skills to stay in touch with me on the regular. He only messaged me via Twitter DM, even though he had my phone number and texting is way easier. I'd message him to see if he was free, and I wouldn't hear back for weeks on end. When I did hear back, it was never an apology or explanation of his absence or any acknowledgment that I'd messaged him. He'd simply write, "How are you?" When I'd see the, "How are you?" in my Inbox, I'd say to myself, "Well, I know how YOU are, Horny." He was gone the entire month of December on a lengthy road trip, and the only way I even knew about it was via his Instagram. As not-his-girlfriend, I knew I had no entitlements to knowing A.'s schedule ahead of time. But as his fuck buddy, I expected at least an answer to my, "Are you around next weekend?" message that sat for ages while, unbeknownst to me, he gave cooking demos three thousand miles away. I don't care how sexually empowered you are, it's still uncool when they don't respond. It definitely doesn't feel at all like friendship, with or without benefits.

We got together once in January, and then he utterly disappeared for six full months. After my third Twitter message went unanswered, I gave up trying to contact him. I knew he wasn't dead, thanks to all the photos of his fucking food (everything is "lit!" *insert eyeroll emoji*). He resurfaced in early July, full of apologies and a tale of woe regarding his ex, and promised to never ghost me again. Which he promptly did the next day, effectively killing any future chance of getting the best head of his life ever again. As I was putting this essay together, weeks into my new thing with the 28-year-old, A. returned from the Land of Ghosts, once again full of apologies and regrets. Because I'm the best sex he's ever had, even if he never wants to be my boyfriend.

I'm sorry I made you feel that way. It was not my intention to hurt your feelings.

I regret now not getting to see you anymore

You scare me because of our physical chemistry

I'll miss our rendezvous and giving you pleasure

Insert a whole row of eyeroll emojis, because jeez.

Sexually potent woman in her prime, yo.

(Laugh about it, shout about it)

But don't think this behavior is exclusive to the Youngs. I've dated plenty of men my age or close enough to it who behave similarly, while also having their own special set of issues. So many alcoholics. SO MANY. Anyone over the age of ten has issues, but the baggage a man in his 40's carries can be filled with criminal records, rehab stints, and erratic work histories. If they're divorced, they have a "crazy ex" who "tries to control their lives" (this is Portland speak for "I am a total pussy"). More than once, I encountered guys who'd broken up with their wives/partners but were still living in the same house because finances were tight. And they're both dating other people but they're still friends and it's not at all weird, except of course it's totally weird. And if they should have kids with said crazy ex, multiply the lack of a spine by a billion. One guy I dated, a sexy single dad with a really rugged manly man job, broke it off with me after his ex saw our pic together on Facebook. This was after telling me how happy he was that things were working out so well with us. I mean, better to find out that he'd conceded ownership of his balls to his ex early on, rather than months into it. But still, nobody enjoys feeling disappointed.

Also, but still, a woman has needs, yo. So if she just can't seem to find any men her age who can muster the energy to keep up with her during the peak years of her sexual prime, can you really blame her for finding herself attracted to what is essentially her male counterpart? Biology is such bullshit. Our bodies mature before our emotions do, and then we begin physically falling apart just as we finally start emotionally figuring out our shit. Women shouldn't have babies until after 40, ideally, but our bodies are all like UH NOPE. Meanwhile, a guy in his late 20's is good to go whenever you need him to, and he probably doesn't have to rush off to pick up any kids in the morning so his crazy ex can go to Silent Yoga or whatever the fuck Portland people do.

(God bless you, please)

So, no men your age want to settle down, and no men not your age want to settle down. Hence the conundrum I find myself in. Hence the going to the movies with D., the cute and funny 28-year-old. Hence the letting him press his shoulder against mine, then melting a little when he raised the armrest so he could hold my hand and run his fingers up and down my forearm. Hence the bringing him back to my house and the divine surprise that followed, where he demonstrated his next level oral skills and I remembered that I can be multiorgasmic when I'm with someone who knows what the fuck he's doing. Hence continuing to see him while basically no one else knows, because if there's anything hotter than fucking a younger man, it's fucking a hotter man on the downlow. Because we work together.

I know, I know, bad idea. But I thought this could be the one time a workplace hookup wouldn't go sideways. Knowing it could only be the fun occasional get together, we agreed to keep the lines of communication open, keep it quiet, and keep it to just us. That was a deal set in stone: no hooking up with anyone else we work with, because that's just beyond disrespectful and would create the kind of drama no one needs. And for a while it was lovely, and it wasn't just super hot sex. We spent a lot of time together not in bed as well, building what I thought was a real friendship that would last well after we eventually stopped with the benefits. He cooked for me. We binge-watched eight episodes of a show I'll probably never be able to finish, because it'll now remind me of how he'd wrap himself around me while we cuddled on my couch. We laughed a lot and shared the kind of intimate details people who have a lot of sex tend to share. One of my friends at work accidentally found out when she saw a text from him, and he told his best friend, but it was otherwise a secret. After about a month of regular hookups, D. started pulling away after the night he told me we'd just had the best sex of his life, which never made sense to me. Suddenly he wasn't as available as he'd been. There was always an excuse that seemed a little off. More than once I asked him if he wanted to keep it going and he said yes. And then I went out of town for a week, with plans to see him once I got back. I texted him upon my return, and he replied warmly that the following weekend would be great.

And then I walked into work the next morning, still jet lagged but looking forward to seeing him. Before I could put my my bag down, one of my coworkers broke the gossip that everyone knew: he'd gotten drunk at a work party and HOOKED UP with another one of our coworkers. To add insult to the broken deal, it was a girl we'd joked about because she is literally the worst at her job and everyone up to our owner knows it. I know I'm far superior at both my job and my blowjobs, so ultimately it's his loss. But still, it was a betrayal, and one I never would have expected from him.

Not only did D. break our deal in the most worst way possible, he let me find out from someone else when he could've told me the day before. When I confronted him after work, he regarded me with that infuriating millennial detachment that I cannot stand, acting like he couldn't have given less of a shit about hurting my feelings. Had it been any other girl on the planet, I wouldn't have cared. But her? I couldn't contain my revulsion. And he wasn't the same person who'd charmed me into bed that first night after the movie. Gone was the sweet and sexy guy who'd sung to me in bed, replaced by this dick who merely shrugged when I asked apparently unanswerable questions like "How could you?", "Why couldn't you have told me?", and "Why HER?!" A follow-up text conversation didn't help much. He blamed it on being drunk, but that doesn't hold water with me when I know they went for food with other people before he took her home with him. He knew what he was doing, and he didn't care how it would effect me when I heard what he did. I can't really wrap my brain around that level of cruelty. And now not only do I have to work with both of them, but now everyone knows about me as well. Everyone is appropriately disgusted by his behavior, but then they also say things like "He's 28, what do you expect? He's a CHILD."

How much do I blame on his age, and how much do I

blame on him just being a dick? And then how much do I blame myself for expecting someone so inexperienced to keep a promise he made to someone who was never going to be his girlfriend? I wanted to trust him, because we'd been friends for months before anything had happened, and I'd always stressed that the Friends part of Friends With Benefits was more important to me. And now thanks to him being this awful, he's ruined both parts of it. He even had the audacity to say, "So . . . this isn't ever gonna happen again?" As if there's a circumstance where I'd allow that. These kids today, I swear!

But seriously, folks. A betrayal like that is a sign from the universe that it's time for me to forget about the Youth of America and start adulting all proper like. I need to start playing with kids my own age, if there even are any. I will always hope to find a true and lasting love, the kind where you know you'll have someone by your side lovingly supporting you for years while your body slowly turns into the equivalent of a bag of wet mulch. A real man who has confidence and maturity and makes me laugh as hard as he makes me come. And really, isn't that what every woman wants at the end of the day?

(Whoa, whoa, whoa.)

RAPHAEL AND THE FRENCH G H O S T AND THE MOON

JENNIFER ROBIN

Pendulous, turned fried chicken brown in the summer sun, I was naked with two men. Eight months grew my ninety-nine pounds to one-fifty. This was not the work of chocolate or militant body-building. I was pregnant.

High Baltimore summer was upon us, a hundred-eight degrees in early July and my flesh-sack could no longer bear clothing. My Buddha-round abdomen grew until the lurid triangle made by my swollen clit and upper thighs was a distant memory. I waddled like a duck, yet persisted in wearing a pair of crimson platform shoes.

Naked, my mind filled with fireworks: De Sade in one hand and a brochure for Lamaze classes in the other, my nostrils assailed by the crotch, the pits, the tears of a man I no longer held, though we still held hands. I was living with my ex-boyfriend, hiding from my family. It was a secret pregnancy.

•

My ex was a masterpiece. I had fallen and couldn't get up. An afro surrounded his head like a dark-matter halo.

He smelled like incense and falafels. He wore Old Spice on his pits, the vintage juice in an opaque glass jar, tinted mushroom, tinted pus. The scent of Old Spice and the feel of pubic hair crackling under my nails, the taste of our tongues against each other, the way we fell backwards in a slick and dizzy airlock release when our foreheads touched. Every pound I gained, every pimple on my face and stain of sweat on my back took me further away from him, from our past.

His name was Raphael. His eyes were congenitally deformed. They released fresh tears every five minutes. With a jaunty Lou Reed reflex, he whipped them aside.

Perhaps because of the tears, and his cop father, and the ska, he developed a street strut that meant he was nobody's fool and every mamma's orphan.

•

We were nineteen. It was natural we had both moved on. I went to France, midnight jaunts with hipsters who slept in attics older than the Sun King, gingerbread eaves. They lived on magic mushrooms and hashish, sang folksongs about wolves.

A fateful sperm impacted my egg and a life began. Raphael was not the father. The father was French.

At first I ignored the changes. Then they became undeniable.

•

As the embryo in my womb grew from pea-size to lettuce-head, I wrote a series of letters to Raphael:

My letter of letters to Raphael was thirty pages, then sixty. I poured into it my emotions about night skies, and wine bars, and the threshold between the familiar and the other. I wrote my unification theory of civilization, and the limits of mind, and the shoes that old ladies wore. I declared my love for him as well, but the letter grew so long that I hoarded it.

It was never sent. Raphael believed I had forgotten him until the phone call, one week before I got on the plane.

•

I took a taxi from the airport and met him at his door, a three-story building on North Charles Street that reminded me of a church.

His floors were swept. His futon was clean. He caressed my swollen gut.

We tried to make love once in this way, but he swam around in there as if his cock had become a tadpole, dwarfed by my dome.

Raphael had a religious awe for my capacity to generate life, but he did not find me attractive.

•

Hours became weeks. I took trips to the welfare office, waited in plastic chairs for WIC vouchers. I'd return with gallons of milk and carrots and pale heads of lettuce and bricks of tasteless cheddar cheese. My rent was babymaking food.

I lounged naked on Raphael's green velvet divan, his oriental carpets, clothes turned to nests, altars of incense and beads. I watched him date a succession of women while stuffing my maw with radishes, cheese curls, tahini skewers, shrimp.

I grew profound, a rose-gold whale with cherry hair. He was a Dylan lyric, the one about a man whose clothes are dirty but his hands are clean.

The summer rose around us like swamp gas: Chesapeake Bay, salty-wet, sidewalks caked in gold dust.

Grass broke through every crack, triumphant. At the fringes of perception, boys ran like lean black glyphs.

I rode the bus, my neighbors so rumpled, so fragrant, glances heavy as prayers. Neon signs advertised ascension between travel agents and typewriter stores:

24-HR PALMISTRY
PAST/PRESENT
FUTURE
DISCOVER YOUR INNER TRUTH:

I bought a banjo on a whim with baby money. It was used. I played it twice but the strings were like acid to my fingertips and the noise was not pleasant to my ears.

I dined in crab shacks: Crack a shell with metal tongs, scoop a fingernail-sized piece of white meat smothered in butter and curry paste, ten minutes invested for a single scoop.

I wasn't sure I'd see the father again, feel his hands on my round expanse.

INSIDE:
A BODY KICKS

I sang on Raphael's fire escape of peeling black paint, banshee harmony to his Lou, his Leonard, his Bob. He'd slink to a corner and paint Icarus, a goddess, figures hooded as my loins, dripping, spongy brown.

I sat for two hours in a bath. My cunt was always there. My cunt, so vast, so wet, so ever present.

I put on clothes when he brought home Veronique.

•

Veronique was a cosmetologist. I envied her skin as dark as vanilla beans, her eyelids painted green as mermaid fins. I envied her ribcage, breasts taut in silky-soft sweater-vests. She grew thick like a bank, like granite and steel and pearl and bombproof glass upon entering the apartment.

Veronique had something I did not possess—the maturity of someone with twenty years on me. She saw through me, she saw through the boy I wished would love me again. She saw through his pile of canvasses and paint-smeared dungarees.

Veronique made Raphael quake and burn like paper.

•

I could not reverse time. I made a phone call to France. I invited the father to live with us. I was eight months done and kept Raphael's company in a bar where a "poet laureate" sat on a stool like an overfed goose and people used the word Bukowski like an incantation.

•

The father was ghost-white. His first day in town he gave a pot dealer thirty-five dollars and the dealer said: "Lemme go down the street and get it. My friend has it. Here, you hold my hat while I go, so you know I'm comin' back."

Tar-black handed ghost-white a straw boater and we watched as his polo shirt and plaid shorts and brown loafers hopped down the street with a wave.

The French Ghost held that hat in his hand for fifteen minutes and burst with rage, swearing so hard that I could not help but laugh and hide my laugh. I was laughing at the only white man on the street.

•

"What ARE you doing here, girl?" Strangers would ask me every day.

"I live here."

And they would ask to touch my stomach and I became holy.

•

Men stopped looking at me. Women asked me if it was a boy or a girl.

I said, "A girl," and did not tell them about the agencies who paid my cab fare to go two hours to Annapolis, or over the Border to Virginia to meet with couples who voted Democrat or didn't write every other word in their essays about how God was Good.

I was grasping at straws. One couple liked Woody Allen movies. They were at the top of my list.

•

We had a cat. She wandered in one day from the fire escape. The French Ghost named her Le Petit Chat. Tiger stripes, green eyes, a wiggle of muzzle and hips on our collarbones. Cans of putrid meat sat opened in the cold-box alongside tasteless cheese.

•

The French Ghost dropped acid. The French Ghost drank candy-colored bottles from the liquor store. One day he took apart an electric guitar to play it inside-out. Screws and springs and ball bearings rolled across the floor and he made a heavenly noise.

The three of us walked hand-in-hand down the streets, singing wildly.

We played jokes on each other. We plotted each other's deaths.

If only the men could break free of their swollen moon. My mass was too great, their orbits pre-ordained.

•

Twilight: Sky looms above tee-vee antennae, rooftop erections of buildings covered in luster, velvet blue.

Raphael caressed my shoulder and asked me to join him in front of his full-length mirror.

He ran his hands across my breasts, slick and slow, down the line of hair, around my womb, fingers lost in the hair, the cunt, and off again. He wrapped himself around my back with tenderness.

"Look," he said. "You have lightning bolts on your belly."

In the mirror: His hair as coarse as a brillo pad against my cheeks, his eyes looking pasted on, my eyes black discs, nose like a deer bending to drink water.

They were lightning bolts, a blue-black in the night. They multiplied every night. Three, eight, fifteen. I looked like a cracked egg, a horror movie thing. And yet I was holy.

He was holding me with his death perfume, his brine.

They were both the father.

●

The doctor handled me like an infected corpse. He said, "I'll pencil you in for an induced labor on the first at 2 pm."

And I said, "No, I have a midwife. I've arranged for a natural delivery."

Her name was Hollis Bagby. She was paid for by US taxpayers. She was tall and blonde and I imagined she spoke the secret language of horses. I was on a waiting list for a delivery room with floral wallpaper.

●

I met a woman at a party who had rainbows in her eyes. She lived on an island with her husband and I offered her my child within two hours of talking to her, eating sugared beets.

•

I had to break it to the Woody Allen couple, no baby for you. They fumed, they fizzled, and restrained their anger, lest I change my mind. They had shown me a room, a shrine to their infertility with a crib and a mobile and educational toys waiting on a dustless shelf.

I was not wrong. I found a woman with rainbows in her eyes, I, a woman with lightning bolts on her womb.

And my thighs, and my breasts. Blue lightning bolts covered my body.

•

I met a photographer at the art school. He drank in our apartment and sang with us into the night. His name was Marty Wozniak and he reminded me of a Violent Femmes Song. He drove a cherry-red convertible that he must have buffed three hours a day to achieve such a crystalline sheen.

I asked if he would drive me to the hospital when I went into labor, and he said, "I have a proposition for you."

I would get a ride at any hour of the day or night if he could do a photoshoot of my birth.

"You've got a deal, sir."

•

The French Ghost was not a bad ghost. His heart was wide, and I was breaking it. This was a gamble, to be in America and watch the woman you love with the child you want to keep and raise in a cabin in the countryside with guitar feedback and lamb roasted on a spit string you along like this, in a land of stingy crabs and smog and men who sell weed with seeds that pop with flame applied.

City of steel, of glass, black skin, monument to industry, concrete heart beats music, fine yellow dust.

•

Outside the food co-op was a woman in her forties who had a shaved head. She met an alien who visited her in an egg. Her father walked through hospital walls. Her arms could turn into moth wings. Her eyes, such a pale blue that they appeared to be made of shaved ice, rolled back in her head. Her entire head was a bloodshot eyeball.

•

I went on a hike with Raphael and the French Ghost and four Lost Boys eight months pregnant and slid down a hill. I slid two yards, but these yards made me feel two miles from my companions.

Lost boys, where are you when I fall? Lost boys, do you think to say: Moon, you should not hike with us. Moon, you have a task to do in the sky.

Lost boys, I am pretending to be a lost boy, too.

Rocks pierced my arm and left two scars. "This is my snake bite," I told lovers for a decade. Over years they faded to white, reminded me of the nights I climbed and drank and spoke of infinity to boys, but they did not want this. They wanted tits, free laughter, someone soft to fall into at day's end, who loved sunsets and didn't scan their eyes like an alien.

I spoke to blue night: "I will never need tattoos."

•

The French Ghost nodded his head when I said it was the best thing to do. He had been to the house of the Woman with Rainbow Eyes.

•

At four AM I woke with contractions. Marty Wozniak arrived disheveled, hair gelled like Tom Cruise but barely, loaded with camera gear, strobe lights, a tower of meters and flares.

The French Ghost was eyes wide, lips like petals. Raphael couldn't decide on a mask for his face, nervous, smiling.

We loaded into Marty's car and sped to Mercy. I was moved to a wheelchair, in the throes of deep breathing, paperwork, blood pressure monitors, stretchers and sheets, stripped to a flimsy gown, turn your body into a C and arch to your left and I chose to do it without painkiller because I wanted to know what a woman feels, I needed to know what a woman feels, what a body does, understand it in my atoms, scream, atoms, breathe, atoms push, Marty Wozniak with a spotlight and two strobes artfully arranged in corners to get the crown of the head as the slit grows wider, almost translucent the skin around the crown, a mat of black hair glistening with spilled amniotic wet.

Meat sandwich of new consciousness and breathing, I see rainbows before I offer this child to rainbows, and if I die now, PUSH, I die for art, the art of LIFE and my nails bite into the hands of The French Ghost, Raphael, they were at each shoulder, both the father, Raphael's tears streaming due to a birth defect and the French Ghost tender and confused and in love and awe, new life in my arms.

Hospital staff cleansed and snipped quickly. Marty got five rolls in two hours.

The new life was taken to the nursery, put in a glass box labeled Baby Girl. I was waiting to fill out the adoption papers. Until then she breathed without a name.

•

For three days nurses wheeled Baby Girl to my room, and one was short:

"There's a note here says you're giving this baby up for adoption. You're heartless. How can you even think of giving up such a beautiful baby? Heartless!"

She grunted and left me to nurse Baby Girl three days of antibodies that come from a mother's milk.

Baby Girl was dense as clay, warm as a furnace. My breasts were gold, the nipples root beer brown.

The Woman with Rainbow Eyes came on the third day with her husband. They asked me a final time if this was what I wanted.

I said yes. I handed them the child and they drove us home: French Ghost, woman who says her life is her own, no matter who it costs.

We sat in Raphael's living room. The French Ghost chain-smoked joints. Le Petit Chat jumped on his lap and he yelled "NO!"

He threw her off his lap and she ran to the fire escape and never came back.

•

For weeks we wandered streets calling for her. Hundred-degree afternoons scanning shadows, hoping to catch a glimpse of a skinny cat with tiger stripes. No luck.

•

"Puh-tee Sha! Puh-tee Sha!"

•

Raphael, the French Ghost, my lumpy self dragging our feet over broken sidewalks, a bushel of ghosts.

•

We watched horror movies. We drank vodka. I ate bags of cheese curls, bulging out of my new uniform: a Mad Hatter t-shirt tucked into a pair of vinyl shorts.

I was a human malignancy. Breast milk crusted my bra. I could not stop bleeding. I bled for a month and filled Raphael's antique iron trash pail with pads until they rotted and he threw the entire pail in the dumpster, along with his paintings.

•

"I give up painting," he said, "I am going to be a Jewish carpenter."

•

The Moon was a crescent, scarred.

We were missing something, the only thing that brought us together. One by one, we escaped.

COME HERE
O F T E N ?

JACQUELINE-ELIZABETH COTTRELL

Just a little before 8:45am on the morning of December 2nd, 2015, I was struck with an almost startled urge to take in my present surroundings.

That Californian-winter's morning found me sitting in a Planned Parenthood located in the Valley-burb of Van Nuys. To date, it had been my fourth time in that specific clinic, but my fifth time utilizing Planned Parenthood's services.

The first had been three years prior.

Shortly after moving to Van Nuys, and moving in with my then-boyfriend, Bry, I decided to that it was time to get equally serious about my birth control as I was my relationship. I switched from my chosen method of the Pill to the Nexplanon implant. Not only did the implant promise protection against pregnancy for up to three years, it was/still is the second most effective form of birth control beneath abstinence, and along with being minimally invasive *(I say "minimally" because of the insertion and removal, which, even then, was hardly what I consider invasive),* I also didn't have to worry about a period *(#yaslawd).*

Because the implant insertion procedure was considered minor surgery, it required a specialist and an appointment that could only be scheduled once I'd had a pelvic exam, the usual STI and pregnancy tests, and a consultation to ensure that Nexplanon would be the best choice for me. This was all done that same day.

My second visit to Planned Parenthood was for the insertion procedure two weeks later. I was so nervous that I had my boyfriend come with me (*or,* it may have been mandatory for him to be there because Planned Parenthood may have warned against driving following the procedure because I was having local anesthesia that would result in the entire deadening of my entire arm—I can't remember which), and despite my knowing prior that he couldn't be with me in the room for the actual procedure, that still didn't stop me from trying to sweet-talk the staff into letting him be present. *(Spoiler alert: They said still said 'no'.)*

For the rest of my duration in the waiting room, I tried not to think about how incredibly dumb it was on my end it to have watched a Youtube video of the actual procedure the night before. Sort of like that other time when I'd made the equally poor life decision to watch *Final Destination 3* for the first time like I wasn't going to fucking Six Flags the next day.

When they finally called my name, I made one last attempt to convince (read: "beg") the kindhearted staff that I needed my boyfriend with me for emotional-support reasons in any—and all—instances of non-invasive minor surgery guaranteed to take ten minutes or less. They still weren't having it, but commended me for trying, and assured me that the "worst" part of the procedure wouldn't be the actual insertion of the implant itself—it'd be was the momentary burning sensation of the local anesthetic they would be injecting into upper, inner arm where the implant was to go.

(And major shoutout to the Van Nuys PP Staff for not only giving me the choice of which arm the implant would go into (as well as wisely suggesting it be my non-dominant arm, i.e. my left one, after I unwisely chose my right one), but also for taking seriously my concerns of the location of the incision and implant being easily accessible when time for later removal and re-insertion, and wouldn't be later covered up by my then-in-process quarter-sleeve tattoo.)

My third visit to Planned Parenthood would occur a few, short years later in 2014, and would include the removal of my implant and return to the Pill (following my breakup with Bry, and subsequent moving back and forth between California and Chicago three times in that short and turbulent timeframe).

The fourth time I visited Planned Parenthood was within days of my return to California after spending another hellish half-year in not-so-sweet-home Chicago, towards the end 2015, in November. Just two months prior, I'd learned I was pregnant by my then-boyfriend of only three and a half months, Nick, of whom I met while at a *supposedly* "Christian" ministry/homeless shetlter in

Chicago, while in rehab for my addiction to benzos and sedatives.

At the time, you couldn't convince me that he (Nick) truly wasn't the man I'd been searching for all my life. After all, the circumstances (to my mentally/emotionally ill and drug-addled brain, anyway) seemed to be *God-blessed*—right down to us sharing the *Same. Exact. Birthday.* I didn't think twice about him being ten years older than me given older men were my *thing*, or that he'd been living at the mission for over a year due to his long-standing history with severe alcoholism, and was presently one of the more notable recovery success stories—

Who else better to understand my struggles and *not* judge me as an addict (or a shitty person in general), than another recovering addict?

After two weeks and a half of knowing one another (and with no thanks to my *other* (former) addiction and dependency to desperately cling to/be supported by to someone—especially in dire times of need), we were saying *"I love you's"* and making plans to leave the ministry after finishing our respective programs, get married, and start a life together that involved children who we swore would never know the brunt of growing up in abusive households as he and I had.

To this day I still question myself over whether or not it was in fact the "deepest" love I'd ever been in, but it was certainly the hardest and the *fastest* I'd fallen for someone—and I only clung *tighter* to him, once the ministry's only "counselor" (and *creator* of the Women's drug and alcohol program) exposed himself as a sexual predator that preyed upon not only myself, but the other young, addicted, desperate, and vulnerable women that entered his carefully constructed and perverted God-based "rehab" program seeking help. His word was law; the head pastors knew this; the staff knew this.

And so, I fully and completely invested myself in Nick to keep myself sane and grounded—I was *desperate* to clutch tight to him as my one, shining hope that in disgusting and corrupt program that touted "God" and "wellness", and to make me believe that my two months in the program so far hadn't been wasted. *God was testing me.* This is what I had convinced myself of; that God had led me to this ministry—not for what I thought was a legit rehab program—but to meet the man I was to be with for the rest of my life.

I meeeeeean . . . *sure*, I grew a *teensy* bit leery once Nick started to confided in me that for the entirety of his year-long rehab program, he had been using his hours-long "trust/day passes" away from the ministry to sneak-drink himself into a stupor, and then come back in time for curfew (but just late enough that no one at the front desks would notice, and if they did, he could play off the drunkenness easily).

However, I could and did overlook, forgive, and keep that secret of his, so long as he continued to tell me I was all that mattered to him in the world.

And sure, I was no longer on/had access to birth control, and even though I knew there was a high-chance of pregnancy, once we started having sex shortly after the *"I love you's"*, I truly believed that I loved this man enough to know that even if I did get pregnant, I would be happy to have his child; and everything would work out just fine no matter what—and that my love (and our child(ren)) would certainly make him quit drinking along whatever other self-destructive habits still had hold of him.

(Spoiler alert: That shit didn't last three goddamned weeks.)

To make a long and painful story short and painful, I found out I was pregnant three weeks later (following a pre-screening pregnancy test prior to dental surgery to see about having my wisdom teeth extracted).

At that point, I was already convinced that I was living in a Godless hell (ie; the ministry itself), so I won't say "things went to hell", however, the events that transpired would set in motion three of the most turbulent and violent three months I'd ever experienced.

The ministry gave us the boot the same morning I went to them (banking on their so-called "Christian" ways/and the fact that I, along with another victim of their *flawed as fuck* "rehab" program, had worked to expose a goddamned sexual predator in their system), and confessed my pregnancy (not like I'd be able to hide it from them in the long-run, anyway).

That very same afternoon, while sitting in a cheap, rundown motel, I watched the *"Heaven-sent, kind, worldly, wise, and loving Man-of-God of whom I'd fallen in love with in a hopeless place"* love-of-my life melt away into absolute nothingness as he proceeded to drink, yell, scream, verbally tear-me-down, and use every, last secret I had confided in him (and no one else) against me.

Even after we had managed to find a stable living situation with his (estranged) sister and her family, his alcoholism and worsening abuse—verbally, emotionally, physically, and sexually—escalated in unspeakable ways. He isolated me from my family, friends, social media, would take and hide my phone, forbid me to talk to anyone, and would often threaten to kill me; to kill my family members, and go to my physically disabled mother's nursing home to rape and kill her, were I to ever "take (his) baby" and leave.

And even when I started to beg him for an abortion early on, his refusal had absolutely nothing to do with skyhigh cost of having one in Illinois, or—it was simply a matter of:

"You kill my baby, and I'll kill you."

And by then the physical violence had escalated to the point where I knew for a fact he was perfectly capable of following up on that threat. During this time, I fell back into my old substance habits; largely to help me cope with everything that was transpiring, but also in the hopes that I would force a miscarriage of my unborn child, of whom by then, I saw as nothing more than an anchor that would forever tie me to a man who would eventually and absolutely kill me and/or it—or both.

Finally, in early November of 2015, I secretly reached out to a couple of friends in California and begged them to buy me a train-ticket back to California for two reasons: the first, was to escape my ex—the second, was to utilize my remaining California healthcare coverage so that I could have an abortion at no cost.

I was in no shape to be a mother; I was damn sure in no shape to carry to term. And I had long accepted the fact that my drug abuse was in all likelihood going to have (if it already hadn't) major adverse effects on my child even if I did carry to term. Several of my family members (y'know—the types who have *all sorts of unhelpful shit to say*—but won't actually help you escape a adangerous situation like that)—suggested that I either *stay* with with Nick, or leave, lie and tell him I had an abortion and keep the child to raise by myself, or put it up for adoption.

And there was no way in hell I was trying to either at the time.

Which—finally—brings me to my fourth and fifth visits to Planned Parenthood. The day after my successful escape back to California, I called Planned Parenthood to schedule an appointment for an abortion. I was already two months along and frantic to abort before I hit the three-month mark (ie, the end of my first trimester), for when it'd be too late.

I was absolutely devastated when I found out that the soonest Planned Parenthood would be able schedule my abortion (following my mandatory pregnancy test/ pre-abortion consultation at a different Planned Parenthood location—ie, my fourth appointment) came with a waiting period of three weeks due to two factors:

One: By the time they could get me in, I would be too far along to utilize the *Abortion Pill* (also known as a *Medical Abortion*), and would have to undergo an *In-Clinic Procedure* (i.e; a *Suction Abortion*).

Two: And because I was having the latter, this required one of two offered choices of anesthesia. I chose Deep Sedation, and this required an anesthesiologist that was only available on certain days.

When I looked at the calendar, I was ready to throw hands, elbows and feet:

The appointment was literally the *day before* the end of first-trimester—but the best they could do. The only relief came from knowing that the abortion would take place at my "home" Planned Parenthood in Van Nuys.

The irony wasn't lost on me.

The next three weeks went by in a dissociative blur, and

I didn't really start to come out of the haze until the day of the abortion. That's when I felt the urge to really take in my surroundings.

Yes. I was sitting in Planned Parenthood for the fifth time in my life. Yes, I had committed myself to having an abortion.

And yes—it was a decision that *saved my life*.

The procedure was nowhere *near* as gory, painful, traumatic, or horrific as I'd too often heard it misconstrued to be. In fact, I'd even go so far as to say it was *almost* a pleasant experience—

And this was due largely in part to the fact that once I'd been admitted into the back of the clinic, given an oh-so-fetch hospital gown and accompanying rolling IV, I was led to sit down in another small separate waiting room where I found myself sitting amongst five or six other young women (equally clad in hospital gowns and attached to IVs).

For almost twenty minutes, the only sound in the room was the small television affixed to the upper right-hand side of the room. It was incredibly awkward until another nightgown-clad woman came in, sat across from me, looked around, and then went:

"So . . . do you ladies come here often?"

That was all it took to catapult us out of a stagnating silence, and into a fit of desperately-needed laughter. The tension shattered and suddenly, we were chatting with one another over and about how and why we each came to convene in this little ole' waiting room for our turns to have abortions. There were several women had traveled as far as New York, Washington, and even Florida to have their procedures done. One girl had even said she was there because the Abortion Pill hadn't worked—which only served to help me to see how fortunate it was that I *couldn't* choose a Medical Abortion.

Once my number was up, I left that small waiting room (gown and all) feeling relieved. Of course, I was still nervous—however, the Van Nuys Planned Parenthood treated me with the utmost respect, humanity, dignity, and compassion.

They didn't ask me: *"Why the hell would you choose to be with a man like that?"*

They didn't ask me: *"Are you sure you don't want to choose adoption?"*

They didn't ask me: *"Why didn't you use any condoms or birth control?"*

They didn't ask me: *"Are you sure you won't regret this?"*

In fact, the staff laughed and joked with me as I laid there on the table, feet up in the stirrups, by calming my fears of the effectiveness of the anesthesia by comparing the strength of the it to *"downing an entire bottle of Merlot"*. I was laughing and *smiling* when I went under. The entire atmosphere was *so relaxed* that you'd have thought I was talking with friends over lunch.

And for that—I will forever be grateful to Planned Parenthood.

Planned Parenthood stood by me before, during, and *after* my procedure with incredible aftercare.

And, when the time comes that I am ready to start planning for parenthood, Planned Parenthood will continue to stand by me (and countless other women) with exceptional prenatal care, resources to parenting classes, and other family planning services—for when I truly will be in a better place to not only have children, but love them, raise them properly, and give them a great future to the best of my abilities.

Planned Parenthood stands for the protection of women, and serves as a safe-haven for us to say, without judgment, ridicule, or shame—*"I'm just not ready to be a parent, yet."*

And this is why I stand with Planned Parenthood.

THE NEW UNNATURAL

JACQUELINE KIRKPATRICK

I just keep driving by sometimes. It hurts too much to stop. Sometimes I know why, but most of the time, I don't. I just drive. Don't even make eye contact. Grip the wheel tighter. Tell myself I have anywhere else but *their house* to go. I have someone else to be. Not her mother. Not today.

I have been a runaway my whole life. My earliest memory of running away is nine years old. But I know it started before that. I remember nine specifically because it was the time my mother didn't flinch, question, or try to stop me when I told her I had to go. She helped me pack my bag. It was a brown paper bag inside of a yellow plastic one. The handles, she said, would make it easier. She gave me a can opener. She reminded me that the last time I ran away I didn't have one and that's why I came back home. I didn't remember that.

Girls are told at a young age that motherhood is the most natural thing; we were *born to do it*, it's *instinct*. Girls are given baby dolls and strollers to mirror their futures in matrimonial bliss. They are shown how to decorate their homes with Barbie dream house templates. They are given Easy-Bake Ovens to get them used to providing for their families. It is all training. It is taking the instinct a step further. It is frosting on the instinct-cake to create a nurturer, a provider, a real woman.

But I was never *that* girl. I had no interest in baby dolls or Easy-Bake Ovens. I was never happy with my Barbies until I got a Ken. Ken represented adventure, someone *else* who existed beyond the dream house, beyond hanging out with Barbie and her bitch friends who were always worried about their hair and clothes, and getting and keeping *girl jobs*, and finding a man so that they could leave their *girl jobs* and have a *family*. I couldn't relate to girls. My goals were different. I wanted to take drugs, drink, have sex, and write poems. I didn't want to go to the dance and sit on the sidelines waiting for the popular guy to ask me out. I wanted to go down to the river and scheme about how to get out of Germantown, NY, small town nowhere, and go find Africa, or India, or maybe just Connecticut. Anywhere. Girls were only allowed to dream of how much of a woman they could be one day.

How *unnatural*. How cruel.

Around twelve or thirteen I began to realize that I didn't have the instinct to nurture or to provide. I realized it would have to be learned. Every day, I have had to tell myself to do both. I have to actively engage every emotion I have because I don't feel it naturally. I know what I'm supposed to do and what is expected of me only because

I have watched movies, and I have seen my peers. My instinct is not to get up, make breakfast, and cuddle on the couch. My instinct is to hide. If I don't understand how I feel I go into panic mode and I seek flight. The fight drive was eliminated long before I have any memory of having it.

When I was fifteen I began to hitchhike. I began to take drugs. I began to wander. I'd leave home for days at a time. I'd call collect from random cities I somehow made it to. Boston. New York. Hartford. Syracuse. My mother accepted every call. She never questioned where I was or why I was there. She just knew. I began to live more on the road, sleeping in my car, or on a Greyhound, than I did in my own bed. I would come home every few weeks to crash. I'd sleep for days. Eat her food. Hold her. Hear her voice. Memorize it. Memorize the lines in her face. Let her memorize mine. We were human together not just "mother and daughter." That's the last relationship I've had that has ever made sense to me. Her unrelenting acceptance of my inability to stay still will undoubtedly be the thing I love most about her.

Then it happened. Something put its roots down in me.

I got pregnant.

I panicked. I read articles on how and why and who and what a mother was supposed to be. I called up other mothers I knew. My family and friends tried to reassure me. They said I'd be so good at it. They said it would all just *kick in*. They said I was caring. Nurturing. Maternal to everyone. I'd be an old pro. I watched my wanderlust best friends settle down, build their changing tables from Walmart or Target and put car seats in their cars. I listened as they contemplated making their own baby food, eating their placentas, and whether or not they would immunize. I shook with fear late at night as the baby turned in my stomach wishing she'd just stay inside. It felt safer that way. Probably for both of us.

When I first met my daughter, it seemed natural. Wait: no, it wasn't. But the love was. Loving her was the purest, most natural thing I've ever done. But love, I know, isn't enough. Human beings can't survive on just love. That was a struggle for me to grasp. It *is* a struggle. If she could just be okay forever on the love I have for her, I know she would have the most amazing life. But she needs other things: food, water, discipline, instruction, structure, patience, guidance. Someone who knows the rules. Someone to tell her to not break them. Someone that will understand consequences and how to deliver them.

I am none of these things. I don't know the rules. Any rule I've ever confronted I've broken while ignoring the consequence.

It all felt so heavy. So I ended things. I left my daughter's father. I left the house we bought together on a dead-end street with a garden and a pool and a two-bay garage. I abandoned the tiki torches at the ends of a deck we sanded and painted so we could have parties with friends for birthdays or Fourth of July. I didn't want to check the mail and sort the bills anymore. I couldn't stand another moment running into neighbors at the local supermarket to exchange stupid hellos, and buy detangler, Lunchables, grapes, and be sure it's 100% juice with no sugar added. I wanted to burn the Google calendar with our schedules regarding parent-teacher meetings, summer vacations, who has to work late, and. . . .

I walked away. If you ask him, though, he'll say I ran.

And maybe I did. I wasn't this *natural* mother everyone tells little girls they will one day get to be if they're really good and kind and beautiful. I became a new version of what natural meant. I embraced being a woman before I was a mother. I realized I couldn't mother, I couldn't even function until I began to figure out *who* I was.

I didn't leave her. I left that life. At first all my friends gasped, and asked if there are any more that I could have done. Therapy? Vacation? Time-off? Medication? Meditation. Remediation. I got emails from family members asking me if it was the *right thing to do*. I wonder if he had been the one to walk away would he have received the same urgent emails and calls? I wonder if he had done it if he would have wept as much?

They stayed in the house we bought together. We made a schedule without the courts based on fair amounts of days and nights. We learned to co-parent. He accepts the person I am and how I function without judgment or question. He understands my love for her exceeds logic and whatever guidelines the world sets up for women when they become mothers. He knows that I need space, and time, and occasionally a reminder that I am doing okay. And I am okay. But there are still days when it's my turn to have her and I begin to panic. Will she like me? Will I like her? Are we okay? Is she okay? Does she know the only thing I understand about us is that I love her?

She climbs into the backseat and buckles herself in. I move the rearview mirror to see her. I ask her how her day was. We talk with silly references to her classmates and popular music. We talk about spelling tests and if we should go bowling or roller-skating. I ask how much she loves me and she replies, "whole world."

Still, I want to apologize to her. I want to tell her that I'm sorry I bleached her Bridgit Mendler t-shirt because I didn't look at the bottle to see that it said "bleach" and not detergent because I was reading Kafka and drinking red wine. I want to tell her that I'm sorry I don't know how to cook chicken, or meatloaf, or a cake from scratch, and that we go out to dinner more than we eat it at home. I want to tell her that I'm sorry that sometimes when it's my day to pick her up I have to drive by because it hurts too much to stop.

But I don't.

"Weird," I say in the mirror, making eye contact, *"because I love you whole world."* And then she'll smile at me with the eyes that are the same color as mine. And that's when I feel like a natural mother.

I'LL MEET YOU IN THE MIDDLE
Impressions of a Life On Tour
DEVORA GRAY

My dear friend said to me, "A relationship has a beginning, a middle, and an end. Stay in the beginning. Once you've reached the middle, you're almost at the end."

He would know. His lover threw himself from the fourth floor of his balcony apartment. He shattered his right leg, shifted his spine, but otherwise lived many years. By the time the end found him, they'd been estranged several years. The lover's father called my friend to say his son had died of a heart attack. He'd survived the fall. It was the thought of landing, having to wait for it, that broke his heart so completely they never found the right pieces to glue back into a shape that could house his loneliness.

To my own self-proclaim, I am a sessionist. Part dominatrix, part wrestler, part sex Sherpa. I take a fantasy—male, female, or otherwise—and break it down into transmutable portions to be explored in reality. I've been on this journey going on ten years, and it's time to say adios, muchacho to something that saved me, fed me, held me when I was weak, and allowed me the space to blossom into the woman I have always wanted to be.

I must do something different, anything different, before I forget there was a time I was not this.

Those are dangerous words. I say them in spite of the spirits clucking their tongues in the waiting room. I have unfinished business. I will not disappear quietly. I will not pretend I wasn't in those rooms, with those people, doing those things. I will not shrink from the harder truths I've created because my image has become too small to house the largess of understanding. I will use them, learn from them, and do my best to remember the beautiful parts of me live in service to others. I focus on one thought, and it comes from a feeling.

Gather your will.

It is the older me, the future me.

I have a loose understanding of the Ego, the Id, and the SuperEgo. Clinical definitions leave me prunish where I long to be plump. My child self is alive and well. For the longest, she's been playing in a solitary room, waiting for me to pick her up from the ugliest daycare imaginable. The present me is the powerhouse and the pivot point. She is in charge of staying aware without prejudice. She can only do this by consulting the child me and the future me. The future me is the drill sergeant. She gives council and prods me into making choices that sound both responsible and uncomfortable. We have pow-wows, usually when I can't sleep. Knowing I can't sleep begins to stir a panic that pushes comfort off the bed. I could use a decent orgasm or a hearty cry. Guess who is in charge of those.

Something happens to me when I'm on tour. I love it and hate it. It breaks off pieces of me I then find in the pockets of the people I meet. For this, I have given myself a year to grow a set. I'll visit my favorite faces, places, and spaces. The why stopped being important the moment I realized it was my last ditch excuse to linger in a place that had become the end.

JANUARY
South San Francisco

They come and go. Some new to me, others old friends. I promised to give myself 45-60 minutes between clients. That's enough to slough off old energy that isn't mine but junk I claim as a hoarder to pad the baseboards.

11 AM: Leg scissor session with facesitting, client requests thong underwear.

I have become the Master of Generalities. I see you on the page and know your life story between the lines. I don't do you justice. If I am quiet, if I allow my mind to go blank, you will arrive, hat in hand, waiting to prove me wrong.

Carbohydrates are frenemies. I keep them in a Baggie, like rocks of cocaine, the unfiltered, uncut platelets highlighting the weather forecast. Every hour, on the hour. Dipping a finger into sweetness, I forget about my thighs.

3 PM. Nap time.

I dreamt I was at home. I came downstairs and thieves had taken my living room. They left the electronics, the most valuable pieces. Two men sat in my kitchen drinking water. They explained, We were hired to pressure wash the driveway. He had your mother's maiden name so we let him in. One was a large black man and he was sad, tired, the way a dishtowel becomes threadbare. The other, a wiry pale man with lank dark hair, was Chinese and something white. A ghost. He stood and handed me a receipt. He said the bill for cleaning the driveway was $38. It was the price of a red dress I wanted and talked myself out of buying. I got mad at him, snatching the slip of paper and demanding he give me a second, can I just have a goddamn minute to process? What's your rush? Smoke a cigarette with me. I'm not a number you got wrong on a test. Anything to feel less violated. The dishtowel told me they'd come at the hours of 2-6 PM when V had not been home. It's my custom to blame her for anything missing, until the lover mentioned her coming home had probably driven them away. V, the girlfriend I never claimed and couldn't own.

7 PM: White widow role-play, client requests to be knocked out by reverse leg scissor but I will show him the rear-naked choke and pressure point varieties

All the places in my body, the ones that make me look away, stop asking to worship them. I know you mean well. I know you only want to please. I know this is not talked about. The seriousness of the situation has pummeled you into fear and that fear lives in your shorts. Instead, ask to worship my mind. Laugh at my jokes.Ease yourself into a puddle, start at my feet, and watch tv while I begin to hum. My pleasure does not live in my clitoris. It is one stop among many.

8:30 PM: Sex chat with boyfriend.

The truth is, I sleep best when alone. I have time to miss him, time to find my own eroticism. We have been juggling the daily. I don't feel pressed upon to make sex the center of our interactions. I feel like I owe my clients something they can hold in their hands if only for a little while. Why is it so different for men? In session, it's cut and dry. It's easy. The men out there, they are desperate to give off a new vibe, to be of use. My stubbornness says, "Do not feed the beast. Starve him." But the starved unleashed eats more than he needs and snaps at his children.

9:00 PM: My darling Ginger Christ, suffocation and philosophical dissertation

John Wayne lives in the heart of us all.

11:00 PM: Wide Awake

I say this to my slave who is my boyfriend for lack of a better title, "I've taken a lover. He's young, too young for me but his eyes are old. He's taller than you but not stronger, not yet. He will watch me smoke a cigarette without blinking. I don't know if he blinks or not. I stare at the ceiling and count the ways nothing in that room reminds me of you. He turns toward me on the edge of the bed, expecting again to be fed, and I can't stop him. I don't want to stop him. I am nothing to anyone but food. It's a lovely feeling."

1:00 AM: Still Wide Awake

If I keep moving forward, I'll catch up to the future I want.

FEBRUARY
Phoenix, AZ

M texted his idea for a potential Arizona bumper sticker: "If the road to Hell is paved with good intentions, the road to heaven is an escalator. A really slow and boring one."

Unlike Vegas men who shop for fruit in the dumpster, these geriatrics subscribe to Christian radio or Detroit rap. An ancient gynecologist asks to be picked up and cradled against my chest. He says there's a certain Amazon lady who can heft him up and close her mouth around his penis. A lifetime of staring at pussy might hypnotize a man so thoroughly he wants to be back in the womb where everything makes sense.

He'll have to settle for the usual lift and carry. He takes this news like a two-year-old. His warbled wrinkles tremble like a thundercloud.

I think the desert has fried his brain. I tell him, "But you don't know where my mouth has been!"

It's the best pacifier I can offer for not wanting to break my back.

MARCH
Columbus, OH @ The Arnold Expo

How to Insert HGH (Human Growth Hormone)

1—Wash your hands and tap the bottle to loosen powder.

2—Swab saline and HGH bottle top with 91% alcohol. Leave the cotton covering the bottle.

3—Insert needle and draw 10 cc of saline.

4—Insert saline into growth. Swirl gently on countertop. Draw 0.5 cc which is the 1 mark on the syringe.

5—Swab skin on tummy with alcohol. Pinch fat and pull away from muscle.

6—Insert at 45-degree angle. Gently hold for a moment and withdraw slowly.

7—Swab skin again to sterilize.

8—Keep HGH refrigerated in Tupperware. Hide all syringes and saline solution. Do not encourage the busybodies with tales of supposed good health.

9—Understand that this is a placebo effect unless prescribed by a real doctor. If you are shooting dead horse, there are worse things to lie to oneself about.

APRIL
Washington, DC, DuPont Circle

We talk of death and the instability of belief in a room impregnated by thunder. I'd open the window it's regulation 4", but the humidity is a third wheel. It will make all playmates jealous. When was the last time I was here? With D and L? It must have been after. Alone and feeling this place, the polo shirt and the neutral business casual, a block away, I am someone different. The beauty is in its tree-lined roundabouts; touristy but elegant and waving the flag. Stars for adventure. Stripes for survival.

Do I do good? If I am good, don't I do good automatically? Monsters are things that refuse to die. They become grotesque and unimaginably brutal not because they were born that way but because they spent too much time being ONE thing and are convinced they can be nothing else. Am I not dark matter balancing the known?

He shares this quote, "I pray death does not find me un-annihilated."

Here, here!

Thistle is the go-to color of charts and graphs. I would call it lavender. It is a shade of violet that is 12% saturated and 85% bright. He says knowing the math takes some of the mystery out of the word. We decide what is appropriate with computational kindness. It's the same as being asked what I want for dinner. I counter with five choices that are acceptable to the other. One or all of them will be right. This extracts the pressure of pleasing both people, a pressure I'm used to, and role my eyes against, that makes my grip too strong and my palm slap against the meat of the inner thigh. I hate to think about all I can do, unknowingly, when I am angry.

I do not fake pleasure, just it's intensity. The pleasure is there as an unwrapped man. His doppelgänger is someplace, smiling, riding the Metro, and can be quickly shoved into a box. On the outskirts of the box, his potential shakes a tambourine.

MAY
Manhattan, New York

We need to go back to the basics. Too much time twiddling the thumbs, and this man will live alone forever. Already in his 50's, never married, no kids. He wants what he wants, and they will chew him up and spit him out. If he lived somewhere else, he'd be happy. I tell him to write down what he wants since conversation of such matters is untenable, painful in a way that makes cattle prods and dildo mouth gags preferable.

He writes:

Surprise take down and control
Tied up
Sensory play—blindfold
touch-tease
NT (Nipple torture)
anal play
Cross dressing—panty stockings
Spanking

No fantasy that says "I like it when my Mistress does this. I feel alive, like Amish furniture." Meaning, he has a problem owning what he wants and what it does for him. This is fine and dandy, but he has no connection to these concepts outside his head. They need to live in his mouth, his other limbs. He's terrified to take charge the same way people who love dogs refuse to adopt one. Instead, they surrogate their friends' animals at parties and take selfies with the whole lot of mutt mixology.

We spend an hour signing him up for match.com. I have missed the blooming of cherry blossoms, yet again.

JUNE
Minnesota/Chicago/Somewhere I Can't Remember

My insides are chewed up bloody. It's sailor knots and bear traps. There is stuff coming down the top of my crown, stuff coming up from the center of the Earth, and it's all getting stuck in the middle. I think the best word for it is constipation, but there's that off feeling. One word to encompass emotional litter is all wrong. It hints at the real condition. I can Google it, sure, but I'm diagnosing the symptom, not the problem. I know what the problem is, and there is no internet cure.

Instead, I meet J at a dungeon called "The Continuum" and proceed to punch a tooth out his mouth. This would cause me great pain had he not asked for it and been filming the Beatdown. Mark Divine says, "Pain is weakness leaving the body." We were going for a version of "The Android Who Dreamed of Electric Sheep."

I meet D for a drive through Morton Arborarium. It comes naturally to look at the wooded fields, the magnolias, and exchange a Red Riding Hood scenario. I got up this morning and hummed a melody that matched the vision of my fist closing in one long swallow around the meat of a fresh heart. The heart didn't belong to anyone specific, but it was male. I couldn't have stopped that fist if I wanted. I felt the muscles as they were mine but the eyes watching stood three feet away.

D says, "I limit my limits to the physical."

My hotel is meant for families. There's a water park attached, but it's closed. I'm bummed. I have a king-sized bed, as this is the best way to wrestle without ending up on the floor. Upon further exploration, I pull back a curtained nook and find a closet-sized cave with bunk beds. I will spend the next three days taking naps in here, legs folded up, pretending I am a child with nothing better to do than dream of dragons and fairies in a wet forest.

There is one thing I cannot do. C asks me to piss on him and use him as the Human Toilet. I've done this before. In Florida, a man with small yellow teeth and flaking skin lies beneath a camping chair with a circular hole cut in the seat. I drink enough tea for a garden party and turn on the tap. I don't mind doing this to him. He's simple. He's still in love with his mother whom he hates. He shoves my foot down his throat until his molars leave impressions halfway up my instep and vomits excess phlegm into a bucket. This is how he uses his social security. Hello, BOUNDARY. He is the opposite of the man I think of now, the one I don't want to know fully because if I did, I would long for him with such fervor, I'd heedlessly construct myself in the image of his ultimate fantasy, a woman whose indestructible nature makes others expendable.

JULY
Denver, CO

When the plane lands, I get in the car. The boyfriend has met me there for a marijuana-filled vacation at the end of a three city 10-day tour. During that time, I've become the wild animal in a cage. I don't give a damn, not a good goddamn about the future we're supposed to build together. I don't remember what I like or what makes me respond. The promises I made to him are faded photographs. What scares me most, I can't feel my gratitude.

I start to cry, "I am not okay." He is a strong man, a big man, a great man, and he cannot help me. Doesn't know where to begin or if I'll ever end. Knowing this is the worst feeling for a man who is capable of carrying baby elephants, I cry harder. It's just a long day, I need sleep, quiet. I need to be myself for a while, not someone's fantasy. Too bad I started out his fantasy. Too bad I thought I'd rather be her and now that's a full-time gig and I can't take it.

That's the problem with this job. You can get too good at it. My work is nothing more and nothing less than reading men like they are books. Some are graphic novels and dime-store thrillers. Some are intricate poems while others are haikus. Some are technical non-fiction or tomes of Moby Dick proportion. Some I skim, while others, ah, the others I never want to put down.

I read them and I change for them. I try to like them all, for there is something worth reading in those pages, I know it. If I can make it to the good part, they will unfold their secrets and I will be blessed. I'll know exactly how to respond and why it's so important.

Maybe it's this kind of joke, that kind of caress. I need to be serious here and playful around that corner. Seduction is not easy; it's a bullet train. After years of dedicated construction, the engine carries you along with one destination in mind. Make no mistake, it's not a shortcut. It is an insatiable beast. Throw yourself off midway and you'll be smeared across a dry lakebed.

The seducer and the seduced are prisoners on this journey. At it's best, it flavors reality, a companion's guide to heart mapping. At it's worst, the fantasy becomes the only reality you wish to know and therefore destined to crush whatever gets in its way.

The boyfriend/slave/childhood brother and I try for normal. We get food, visit a weed shop, and I fall into bed, a very nice, pillowy bed in a hotel he's handpicked for the ambiance of grand downtown, feeling as useful to the human race as a refrigerator condiment.

The next three days are a vacation on how to break up with a person who can no longer be my best friend or my lover and certainly not my slave. There's no help for it. Choosing myself often means failing another and learning to be okay with that.

JULY
Philadelphia, PA

To the boy-man somewhere in New Jersey, I get that you workout 4x a week. To boast that I've never had a client like you, and this session above all sessions shouldn't be missed, is boldly offering information that will be used against you. As if there were a shortage of young men with too much energy, too much free time, I offer this gentle advice: Crack a book, mofo. Lots of books. Spend your weekends at the library. Goodreads has groups worth joining. They'll turn you on to some hum-dingers that can hurt/heal you in ways I wouldn't get atpicking you apart for two years straight. You think you're worth that time investment, of course you do. You're young. If you offered me prey with a body and a mind? I'd go after that for free. Why? Because I have too much energy and too much free time.

•

Definition of a badass bitch:

Noun: feminine in energy; one who must at various junctures inspect the image of the self and the perceived image to determine if they are friends.

ALSO: a person whose will is greater than the fear of change and resulting hardships.

ALSO: the protector, the warrior, the creator of cavernous spaces; the conductor of mass potential and synergetic action

ALSO: MAMA-FUCKING-BEAR

Example:

Verb: the action of ingesting a handful of male showmanship, assumptions, perceptions, and misunderstandings, assimilating the information, dividing the data into categories (a) useful (b) irrelevant (c) utter bullshit; then up-chucking the newly structured deluge with biting precision in a verbal spew of lengthy and quantitative proportions, usually directed at one person but including a long list of predecessors.

ALSO: taking back one's power

ALSO: MAMA-BEAR-RANT

Example: "Let me tell you about yourself."

AUGUST
Atlanta, GA

As I grow closer to my roots, a man with one leg gives me a run for my money. He's a tougher wrestling partner than anyone westside, except for the lumberjack in Alaska who sends me fresh salmon. The strongest I've grappled, they come from Austria, Norway, and Eastern Europe. They do not depend on their electronics or supplements. They are lean, flexible, and made of steal. The amputee squeezed the crap outta me.

Scarlett Devine is getting old. I know it's time to hang up my boots when a 28-year-old client, previously addicted to nasal spray, tells me he's been watching my videos since he was 18. I've begun concocting alternate egos. So far, I can be:

Farlett Bovine, all-American beef-cake.

Faltula the Stripper, giving a whole new meaning to fire dancing. No lighters please.

Artisan Odoressa, stinkiest cheese-eater of the West.

Fuck the FDA's food pyramid. I miss my Nanny's cooking.

SEPTEMBER
Los Angeles, CA

Does the Universe abhor a vacuum? I see an empty cabinet; I fill it with towels, toys, and get distracted. Where did I put my vibrator? Is it still under the pillow? Enough is never enough until you've had too much. The Universe likes to play tricks on me. It has a wicked sense of humor. I give it a nod, brevity being the soul of smartass.

The worst for me is substituting feelings. I don't feel a certain way, a way I'd like to feel NOW, so I take something. Maybe it's a swig of coke, a pre-workout drink, a fat-burning supplement. Maybe I take a drag of smoke or a hit off the vape. I take something small that fits in my hand like a baby bird. I don't feel like I wish to feel, but I am assured to feel that way by addition.

Addiction. Addition. The knowingness that relief is on the way acts before the addictive's chemical reaction kicks in. The placebo effect. I want an outside force to "spot me." Maybe the truest definition of addiction is "to add to that which is already full in hopes of attaining a feeling not realized without the royal fuck-up of being who you are not."

Where does the power live? It is an extension from the point in my center flowing out the length of my arm and into the substance I am fixated. This e-cig, for example. The power I seek from it? To calm and dispel my anxiety. Should I choose to focus on one part of this equation, I'd pick the action, not the additive. Chemistry works, yes.

One is a quick drain that doesn't replenish what it extracts. It is the act of throwing something away as if it's bad, unwanted, unnecessary, and disruptive. The other is the act of push and pull. Circulation. I push away energy and then pull it back. It's an awareness that energy is needed, flexible, moldable, and transverse. We contract to lengthen. We push & pull to stabilize the center.

The addictive by itself is nothing. A mass, a thought, a whimper, and a bang.

I want clean energy. I want flexible strength. I want confidence and ease. I want grace. I want them NOW. Like the baby, too spoiled by the world around her, I am demanding what I know to be true. I find it unacceptable that I go without. No one does that to me. How dare they? Who are they?

Those within reach.

Whoever invented the boomerang must have had intrinsic knowledge of this energy system. It was a child playing with sticks. It was not pampered and spoiled. It was trusted and told to shoo, explore, cope, and find ease in the mind, the space, the Nature around it. That child knows when to distract and when to settle into silence.

I must find that child, hidden inside large bodies changing too slowly to be anything but adults. It was ignorant of me to think I could start or stop such a thing, abrupt as an overpass in a deluge.

There she is again, the future me with a command, Gather your will.

OCTOBER
Pittsburgh, PA

I'm overly sensitive about being outwardly superior. There's a complex at work, for sure. Outside/inside validation, why can't they act as collaborators? What I have now is SPY vs SPY. I'm waiting for one of my cherished clients. I don't like calling him a client. He feels somewhere between friend and insect. I'm about to drain him while he wiggles frantically in the web. I like the wiggles. It gives me that sign, Hello? There IS life in there!

Over the years, both consensually and not, because let's be real, half the shit we do, we don't know we're doing on the up-and-up. This has become the dance of parallel universes. I know him as he knows me. Somewhere else, we are married. We meet here briefly to say, "You are never gone." The work of this life is with another, many others, and the same goes with our respective mates. It's a nice feeling, an arranged marriage where love took root and grew, like nostalgia.

That idea, that we are one and there is no separation between us, is the perfection of love. I savor it on my tongue like a lemon drop, but try bringing that up in casual conversation? I get a better response when I ask, "When's the last time I was in this room, and did I ever leave?"

We both know to let it lie and exit stage left. He, and many others like him, have given me the courage to say Goodbye the right way. I cannot image doing what others have done; changing my number, disabling my website, vanishing like they were nothing more than dust on my tires sprayed off in a discount carwash.

I created this world, not the other way around. It is not allowed to get the best of me or extinguish the gift of their vulnerability.

NOVEMBER
Baltimore, MD

Two days into a this trip, the east coast is hit by a blizzard. I'm stuck in The Westin. I hadn't realized they prep for this sort of thing and will not have to ration protein bars or rely on a stipend of vending machines jelly snacks and bread product.

Watching it come down from my bedroom window, I'm hit by the wonder, the wall of white that is my mind, my heart, my box. I start to cry and it is a wave deep in my belly rising from my pelvic floor. It's pent-up stress, isolation, perfectionism, adrenal fatigue, all that jazz. Knowing the symptoms alleviates my sense of time, nothing more. I say out loud, "I don't want to do this anymore."

Poor little girl. The straw has snapped. There's no going back now that I've come to the middle but cannot see the end. It's just white noise. How to go back to normal? I know this space. This is my kingdom, the bedroom, the fantasy, the charade, and the grace. I don't know what detritus I'll keep and what I'll leave behind.

The end is nigh, as they say. I still don't know who "they" is, but I do know if I met them, I'd either shake their hands or spit in their faces. I'm left with the impression that they are prepared for both. My will, gathered up like firewood and stacked by the door, Mama Fucking Bear says sweetly, "Grab your bags. We're going home."

DECEMBER
Las Vegas, NV (Home Sweet Bitter-After-Taste)

I see you looking at me in the elevator. I feel the whites of your eyes. You know what that means? I can hear your heart palpitating. Predators lust for that moment. I wear animal print and a shirt that says, "I Hate Running."

I want to turn to you, ignoring the husband, and ask, "Why are you afraid of a penis?"

"Did you say penis?"

"A penis. Is it fear or something else?"

"No. I just don't like the look of it."

"Sleeping or awake?"

"I don't stare at it!"

"If you could, peel back the sheets. Watch it sleeping. See how vulnerable it is? You were taught a fear that doesn't belong to you. That penis? It's a thing of beauty. Love the skin, the chambers, the nerve endings. Make no mistake. The man attached puts great value in what it does, how it feels, and what it wants. But that penis, he's on your side. He may like looking at me, but he gets to belong to you. Go make friends. Your husband never has to know."

People don't fear or hate my kind because we are immoral or unethical. My power isn't in what I can make a man do, say, or feel. We influence without force. We manipulate awareness and with it, control. We hold sacred the moment "I" and "me" become pinpricks on the Universal map.

Their fear is in vain. I don't love the cock because I can control it. I don't need it's validation to tell me I am WOMAN. I've seen every size and shape. It doesn't frighten me. I don't have to touch it, mount it, smother it, or suck it dry to stand for something bigger than an old shoe. It was not in greed or covetousness I stroked the shaft of ignorance. With every wrestled orgasm, quaking wet tide, and exclamation, I lay witness to the small death and winked at the shadows. Here is the suspension of time, thought, singularity, and ego. Here is LIFE.

In each exhausted expression, a reminder as Death smiles, "There is nothing to fear. I'll meet you in the middle."

Who knows what I'll do next. This is only the beginning. Gather your will.

ABOUT THE AUTHORS

BOODAWE is an Indigenous Switch Femme from Los Angeles that takes no shit and makes mean tacos. This is her first published piece.

Born in Chicago, IL, JACQUELINE-ELIZABETH COTTRELL is a Pangender and Pansexual model, suicide survivor, nerd, gamer, an active Cosplay Deviant and former SuicideGirl, and along with writing for *Afropunk*, *BlackGirlNerds*, and a slew of other media sites, she represents the Black-owned, creative entertainment company, *Noir Caesar*, as their Entertainment Representative and Spokesmodel. She hosts bi-weekly vlogs that discuss Black nerd culture, and keep fans informed on what's happening within the company. She is presently writing a script for a brand new comic-book title to be featured in a future edition of the company's monthly, serialized publication,

Hype Monthly Magazine, similar to *Shounen Jump* and *Shoujo Beat*.

TARA DUBLIN is a single mom, writer, and voiceover actor. Originally from New Jersey, she currently lives near Portland, Oregon. Follow her on Twitter (where she was among the first to be blocked by Donald Trump) and Instagram @taradublinrocks

SABRINA DROPKICK is a multi-hyphenate artist, fat activist, and Antioch University Master's candidate studying Clinical & Applied Community Psychology. She founded and organizes the San Fernando Valley Zine Fest and self-publishes her own zines including the ongoing memoir *Celibate Slut* on addiction and mental illness. She hosts a free monthly open mic for writers and musicians at Book Show in Highland Park and skates as Philly Sleazesteak with SFV Roller Derby. Originally from Philadelphia, she now lives in Van Nuys, CA with her roommatesisterchild Leslie and Sir Gandle-"The Best Fucking Cat Ever"-tron.
@sabrinadropkick
www.sfvzinefest.com

AMBER FALLON lives in Massachusetts with her husband and two dogs. A techie by day, horror writer by night, Mrs. Fallon has spent time as a bank manager, motivational speaker, produce wrangler, and butcher. Her obsessions with sushi, glittery nail polish, and sharp objects have made her a recognized figure. Amber's publications include *The Warblers*, *The Terminal*, *Sharkasaurus*, *Daughters of Inanna*, *So Long and Thanks for All the Brains*, *Horror on the Installment Plan*, *Zombies For a Cure*, *Quick Bites of Flesh*,

Operation Ice Bat, and more! For more information, please visit her at www.amberfallon.net.

DEVORA GRAY is a writer, traveler, and sexpert comic. She is the creator and host of *Dear Sweet & 'Lo*, a YouTube advice column specializing in the Art of Fantasy, and author of *Human Furniture and the Quest for the Perfect Woman*. She lives in Las Vegas, NV.

MP JOHNSON is a lady first and trans second. No, actually, she is a lady first and a writer second, and trans . . . Wait, no, she's a lady first, a daughter and sister and aunt second. Writer is definitely in the top five, and trans is probably somewhere a little lower than that, just above cereal connoisseur. It's part of her, but probably doesn't define her as much as other people want to use it as her defining trait. Oh, and about the writer thing: She's the Wonderland Book Award-winning author of *Dungeons & Drag Queens*, *Berzerkoids*, *Nails* and many other books. Her short fiction has appeared in *The Dark*, *Dark Discoveries*, *Year's Best Hardcore Horror* and many other publications. She has created a variety of zines, including fifteen issues of Freak Tension. She is the founder of Weirdpunk books, a press devoted to merging punk rock and genre fiction.

Learn more at www.freaktension.com.

R. J. JOSEPH is a Texas based writer and professor who must exorcise the demons of her imagination so they don't haunt her being. A life-long horror fan and writer of many things, she has recently discovered the joys of writing in the academic arena about two important aspects of her life: horror and black femininity. When

R. J. isn't writing, teaching, or reading voraciously, she can usually be found wrangling one or five of various sprouts and sproutlings from her blended family of 11 . . . which also includes one husband and two furry babies.

R. J. can be found lurking (and occasionally even peeking out) on social media: @rjacksonjoseph

https://rjjoseph.wordpress.com/

DIANA KIRK is the author of *Licking Flames: Tales of a Half-Assed Hussy* and has been published in *Nailed, The Progressive, Five 2 One* and *Yellow Mama*. She writes everything from business essays to sexy fiction but her most comfortable space is in deeply personal, edgy, and aggressive words. After working for years as a real estate investor, she's now the owner of several businesses on the coast of Oregon including a 91 year old bar on the coast of Oregon called Workers Tavern. All of which sounds cooler than she really is since most days she's hovered over a computer knee deep in spreadsheets or essays for her next book titled *Sucking Wind*.

JACQUELINE KIRKPATRICK is a writer living in Upstate, NY. Her work has been published in *Creative Nonfiction, The Rumpus,* and *Thought Catalog.* She is a graduate of the now-murdered M.F.A. creative writing program at The College of Saint Rose in Albany, NY. Check out her work at jacquelinekirkpatrick.com.

KATHRYN LOUISE is a 26-year-old writer, photographer, model, and filmmaker living outside Seattle, WA. Kathryn graduated from the Evergreen State College with a degree emphasizing creative writing and media studies in 2017.

Kathryn is a current MFA candidate at Pacific University and the author of *The Blacklist* (Clash Media, 2017) and *Death and the Blue Blood Blues* (Great Jones Street, 2016). Find her online at www.kathrynlouiseh.com or on Instagram and Twitter as kathryn_louiseh.

JESSIE LYNN McMAINS is a writer, zine-maker, and the 2015-2017 Poet Laureate of Racine, WI. Recent publications include 10 Poems By, an e-chapbook published by Hello America, and *It's Like The 'Watch The Throne' of Tender Punk Poems*, a split chapbook with Misha Bee Speck. She's the owner/editor of Bone and Ink Press, a small press with the aim of publishing limited-edition chapbooks of poetry, non-fiction, and experimental genres, written by marginalized writers. She also teaches workshops on memoir, poetry, and zine-making. You can find her website at recklesschants.net.

CERVANTE POPE is music and cultural journalist currently based in Portland, Or. Having recently turned 28, she spends her time avidly loving animals, heading to shows and trying to navigate around town and a world where she's not always welcome. Her work has been featured in a variety of outlets from the *Portland Observer* to *PQ Monthly* but look out for her music pieces in the *Portland Mercury* and *Willamette Week*, as well as her takes on metal over at mxdwn.com.

JULIE REA's work has been published in several places, including *The Intima: A Journal of Narrative Medicine, Vol. 1 of Mosaics: A Collection of Independent Women*, and most recently in *Nude Bruce Review* and in *BLYNKT*. Her work will appear in *The Weird Reader* later this year. She is a graduate of the City College M.F.A. Creative Writing Program and currently lives in the Philadelphia area and writes about life in a wheelchair and other fascinating subjects. You can find her at @phillylitgrl and https://www.juliereawriter.com

JENNIFER ROBIN IS raw power, wears extra mascara, seeks escape velocity. She booked and hosted a live avant-garde variety show, *Night of the Living Tongue*, on Portland's KBOO 90.7 FM, from 1999-2008. She has toured the country with a mix of performance art, music and reading, including appearances at *Bumbershoot*, the *Olympia Experimental Music Festival,* and Portland's *Nofest*. Her work has been featured in *Plazm*, *Five2One*, *Gobshite Quarterly*, *HorrorSleazeTrash*, and *Ladybox Books*. Her collection of non-fiction vignettes, *Death Confetti: Pickers, Punks, and Transit Ghosts in Portland, Oregon*, was released by Feral House in 2016. An intimately surreal exploration of America, *Earthquakes In Candyland*, will be released by Fungasm Press in 2018.

ROCKET has been entertaining Rose City audiences for ten years as stripper. She now travels and performs as a burlesque entertainer and producer (Go Go Rocket Productions), and is one of the founders of *Sign of the Beast Burlesque*, a troupe that performs exclusively to metal music.

The first two volumes of her zine series *They Call Me Rocket: Stories of a Rose City Stripper* can be found in her online store: https://www.etsy.com/shop/TheDahllHaus

ELEANOR ROSE is the founder of *Empowered Muses*, an online resource for freelance models that demonstrates passion and commitment for bringing education, resources, and a voice to the model community. She is also a mentor and coach that helps freelance nude models who are tired of getting all the wrong gigs make plenty of money doing what they love. A nude model herself, her work has been shown in the Louvre and on Playboy TV. You can find her online as a model at www.eleanormodel.com and as a coach at www.empoweredmuses.com

MISSY SUICIDE is the founder and creator of *SuicideGirls.com*. She has seen a lot living her life online for the past 15 years, and firmly believes that confidence is the sexiest attribute a person can have. She currently resides in Los Angeles, CA.

KIM VODICKA: Poet. Benevolent Nihilist. Spokesbitch of a Degeneration. Beavis in Scorpio. Moon in Roseanne. Penis in Uranus. Venus in ASS GLAM! She is the author of two poetry collections: *Aesthesia Balderdash* (Trembling Pillow Press, 2012) and *Psychic Privates* (White Stag, 2018 [forthcoming]). She is also responsible for the *Psychic Privates EP*, a poetry chapbook on 7" vinyl (TENDE RLOIN, 2017), as well as the *Psychic Private*s comic book series (Oily Pelican Press). Her poems, art, and other abominations have been featured in *Spork*, *Epiphany*, *Industrial Lunch*, *Smoking Glue Gun*, *Luna Luna Magazine*, *Paper Darts*, *The Volta*, *Tarpaulin Sky*, *Makeout Creek*, *Mojo*, *Best American Experimental Writing* (BAX) 2015, and many others. Cruise her at kimvodicka.com.

FURTHER COPYRIGHT INFO & ACKNOWLEDGEMENTS

ABOUT THE EDITOR

Tiffany Scandal is the author of the novels *Jigsaw Youth* and *Shit Luck*, and holds a degree in Feminist Studies from UCSB. She has modeled and worked as a photographer for Suicide Girls, and as a social worker, providing counseling services for at-risk women and LGBTQ youth.

For their additional generosity, we would like to mention Sonya Cheney, Fred Childs, Sam Cowen, Scott Emerson, Rob Hart, Austin James, Ian Muller, Teresa Pollack, Liv Rainey-Smith, Sam Richard, Michael Smith, Curt Sobolewski, and Craig Young. We would also like to thank everyone who pre-ordered this book as well as the authors who participated in it. You are amazing.

Thank you for picking up this King Shot Press title. We are a small press based in Portland, Oregon, dedicated to the publication of fine works of prose and poetry. If you loved reading the book you hold in your hands, do please tell your friends about it. For more information about us, see www.kingshotpress.com.

AVAILABLE FROM KING SHOT PRESS

Leverage by Eric Nelson
Strategies Against Nature by Cody Goodfellow
Killer &Victim by Chris Lambert
Marigold by Troy James Weaver
Noctuidae by Scott Nicolay
I Miss The World by Violet LeVoit
All-Monster Action by Cody Goodfellow
Nasty (ed. Tiffany Scandal)
The Deadheart Shelters by Forrest Armstrong
Drift by Chris Campanioni
Killer Unconquered by Chris Lambert

CPSIA information can be obtained
at www.ICGtesting.com
Printed in the USA
FSOW03n0045230218
44730FS

9 780997 251883